One World Language

Media & Culture

Brian Devine

MEDIA & CULTURE
LISTENING AND SPEAKING

Published in 2021 by One World Language U.S.A., Inc.
1830 Martin Luther King Jr. Way, Seattle WA, 98122

E-mail: oneworlddevine@gmail.com
Website: www.oneworldkorea.com

Printed edition available for order through oneworldkorea.com/contact-us.html

Media & Culture Beginner (Levels 1 - 2)

Lesson Length: **50 - 90 minutes**

Number of Lessons: **30 lessons**

Hours of Instruction: **25 – 45 hours**

Overview

Media & Culture is a discussion class for students who have a basic background in English and wish to expand their speaking and listening skills by gaining a deep understanding of the English-speaking world through both language and culture. This curriculum uses materials from a variety of sources including American TV series, Youtube videos, and movie clips to generate topics for discussion. Each lesson includes a focus on grammar or useful phrases to help students apply grammatical rules in speaking like the native speakers in the video clips.

Class Preparation

Students are strongly encouraged to preview videos before each class. These videos can be found by accessing the website links below as well as answer keys to the listening comprehension for students to self-check. Teachers are encouraged to use a portion of class time to review and check comprehension, but the majority of class time should be focused on putting vocabulary and idioms into use through discussion of the material.

Links to Videos:

https://www.oneworldkorea.com/mc---beginner---session-1.html

https://www.oneworldkorea.com/mc---beginner---session-2.html

https://www.oneworldkorea.com/mc---beginner---session-3.html

Table of Contents

Session 1

Session 2

Session 3

Lesson 1: New Roommate

Warm up: Introduce yourself by answering these questions...

- What is your name? ➔ My name is…/I'm…/You can call me…
- Why are you studying English? ➔ I am studying because I want to…

Vocabulary

Introduce	Everybody	Land
Hometown	Gonna (going to)	Move
Hobby	Roommate	Couple
Married	Nice	Ago
Single	Pretty	Either
Children	Last name	Unpack

Listening Comprehension  https://www.oneworldkorea.com/mc---beginner---session-1.html

Watch First: As you watch the video**, listen and try to get the main ideas.**

- Why is Joey introducing Janine to his friends?
- Where is Janine from?
- What is Janine's job?
- Does Joey know Janine very well?

Listen for Details: Now listen again and fill in the blanks with vocabulary words as you listen.

Joey: Hey everybody! I'd like you to meet Janine. She's gonna be my new ________________!

Ross: Hi.

Janine: Hi.

Joey: And she's gonna ________________ with me!

- Why do you think Joey is so excited to introduce his new roommate to his friends?

Monica: It's nice to meet you. Janine…?

Janine: Le Croix. Janine Le Croix.

Joey: I didn't know that. What a pretty ________________.

- Notice Monica's tone when she says Janine's name. We can use this tone to hint the question, "what is your last name"? Try this tone to ask your classmate's last name.

Chandler: So where are you from?

Janine: Australia. I just moved here a ______________ ______________ ago.

Joey: From the land down under? I didn't know that _________________!

- Why is Joey's reaction to this information funny?

- Did you have a roommate before? Did you have a close relationship with them?

Ross: So, uh, what do you do?

Janine: I'm a dancer.

Joey: You're a dancer? She's a dancer!

Janine: Well, I think I'll go and _______________.

- Why do you think Joey is so excited about Janine's job?

- Do you think it is okay for single men and women to be roommates?

<u>Grammar Focus</u>

1. "Be" Verbs

✓ Verbs must match with the subject of the sentence.

✓ Negative sentences need "not" after the "Be" verb.

✓ The verb comes first in questions

Subject + Verb	Subject + Verb + Negative	Question
I am Korean.	**I am not** American.	**Am I** in the right class?
It is my hometown.	**It is not** my home now.	**Is it** your first English class?
He is excited.	**He is not** bored.	**Is he** bored?
She is a dancer.	**She is not** a singer.	**Is she** from France?
You are single.	**You are not** married	**Are you** married?
We are adults.	**We are not** children.	**Are we** late for class?
They are friends.	**They are not** lovers.	**Are they** dating?
You are my classmate.	**You are not** my roommate.	**Are you** my coworker?

<u>Practice Part 1:</u> In pairs, interview your partner with yes/no questions using Be verbs. Take notes about their responses.

1. Are you a person with blood type A?

2. Are you married?

3. Are you studying English for the first time?

4. Are you working in the city?

<u>Practice Part 2</u>: Now the other classmates should ask you about your partner by changing the questions above to use "Is he/she...?"

Example: "Are you a person with blood type A?"

➜ "No, he is a person with blood type B."

2. WH- Questions: Who, What, Where, Why, When, How

✓ These words can be added to the beginning of yes/no questions

✓ "do/does" is often used with questions that use another verb

✓ Clarifying words can be used with "How" (ex. much, many, long, often, far, old) and "What" (ex. type of, kind of, time)

✓ Possessive nouns (his, her, your, my, their, our, its) can be used when the object is a noun

Wh- word	Using "Be" Verb	Using "Do" with other verbs
Who	**Who is** that?	**Who do** you **like**?
What	**What is** his job?	**What does** he **do**?
Where	**Where is** her office?	**Where does** she **work**?
Why	**Why are** they sleepy?	**Why do** they **want** to sleep?
When	**When are** you free?	**When do** you **have** free time?
How	**How are** you feeling?	**How do** you **feel**?

<u>Practice Part 1</u>: In pairs, interview your partner using these Wh-questions. Take notes about their responses.

1. Where is your hometown? ➜ My hometown is…, but now I live in…
2. What are your hobbies? ➜ I like to …
3. When do you go home? ➜ I go home …
4. How are you feeling today? ➜ I am feeling…
5. Why do you feel that way? ➜ I feel that way because…
6. Who is your favorite person in the world? ➜ My favorite person is…

<u>Practice Part 2</u>: Now the other classmates should ask you about your partner by changing the questions above to use "is he/she" OR "does he/she"

Example: "Where <u>is his</u> hometown?"

➜ "<u>His</u> hometown <u>is</u> Seattle but now <u>he lives</u> in Paris."

<u>Extra Activity</u>

We will play a guessing game in small groups. One person in the group will think of a famous person but will keep it a secret. The other students will take turns asking questions to find out more information about this person. The student who guesses first gets to choose the next famous person.

<u>Remember to...</u>

- ✓ Choose a famous person who everyone knows well.
- ✓ Wait for your turn to ask your question.
- ✓ **Ask and answer in full sentences!!**

<u>Example Questions...</u>

- ☐ Is it a man or a woman?
- ☐ How old is he/she?
- ☐ Is she an actress/singer/politician/CEO?
- ☐ What country is he/she from?
- ☐ Is he/she married?

You can take notes on questions and answers here...

Question	Answer

Question	Answer

Question	Answer

Question	Answer

Lesson 2: Superpower Show

Warm up: What is a skill or hobby that you can do?

Vocabulary

Code	Mysterious	Survive
Government	Darwin	Cover
Agent	Fit	Stage name
Secret	Adapt	Fly

Listening Comprehension  https://www.oneworldkorea.com/mc---beginner---session-1.html

Watch First: As you watch the video, listen and try to get the main ideas.

- Why does Mystique want to make code names?
- What can each of the characters do?

Mystique	Banshee	Alex
Darwin	Angel	

Listen for Details: Now listen again and fill in the blanks with vocabulary words as you listen.

Mystique: We should think of code names. We are government ______________ now. We should have secret code names. I want to be called Mystique.

Banshee: Damn, I wanted to be called Mystique.

Mystique: Well tough, I called it. I'm way more ______________ than you. Darwin, what about you?

Darwin: Well, uh, Darwin is already a nickname and you know, it sort of __________. Adapt to ________________ and all. Check this out. Thank you brother, thank you. What about you?

- If you could change your appearance like Mystique, who would you change into?
- What dangerous jobs could a hero like Darwin do?

Banshee: Cover your ears. Your turn.

Angel: My -- ah -- ________________ name is Angel because of this.

Mystique: You can fly!?

Angel: Uh-huh. And um...

- Where would you fly, if you could fly like Angel?

Darwin: Alex, what is your gift? What can you do?

Alex: It's not, um, I just can't do it. I can't do it here.

Darwin: Can you do it out there?

Angel: Why don't you just do it out there? Come on!

All: Alex, Alex, Alex... Hey!

Alex: Get down when I tell you. Get back. Whatever...

- Which character would be a good government agent?

Grammar Focus

1. Expressing Ability with CAN/CAN'T

Y/N Question	Answer	Sentence	Wh Question	Answer
Can you swim?	Yes, I can.	I can swim.	- Where can you swim? - How fast can you swim?	- I can swim in the pool. - I can't swim very fast.
Can you drive your car?	No, I can't.	I can't drive my car today.	- Why can't you drive your car today? - When can you drive your car?	- I can't drive my car because it is getting repaired. - I can drive my car after 5:00pm tomorrow.

✓ Use the infinitive after 'can'. For negatives add "n't" or "not".

Practice: In pairs, ask a Y/N Question followed by Wh Questions using the verbs below.

- o Play a musical instrument
- o Go snowboarding
- o Run fast
- o Go Swimming

- o Drive a motorcycle
- o Ride a Bike
- o Drink a lot of alcohol
- o Speak another language

2. When to use "PLAY, DO, & GO"

PLAY	Generally used with games and activities that have a ball.	Golf, soccer, basketball, tennis, badminton, chess, video games
DO	Used with activities that stay in one place	Boxing, yoga, palates, stretching, homework
GO	Used with activities that move from one place to another.	skiing, swimming, running, hiking, horseback riding, Scuba diving, camping, shopping

Example Dialogue:

Do you like <u>golf</u>?

Yes, I love to <u>play golf.</u>

Can you <u>play golf</u> this weekend?

Sorry, but I can't. I am <u>going horseback riding this weekend.</u>

Okay, maybe another time!

Role play: Invite your partner to an activity by changing the example above.

Do you like _________________?

Yes, I love to _______________.

Can you _____________________________?

Sorry, but I can't. I am _______________________________________.

Okay, maybe another time!

Discussion

If you could have a superhero skill, which skills would you want? Rank the top 3 skills that you want. Then explain why you want those skills by telling what you "can" do with that skill.

<table>
<tr><td>☐ Invisibility</td><td>☐ Being Super Strong</td></tr>
<tr><td>☐ Self-healing</td><td>☐ Seeing through walls</td></tr>
<tr><td>☐ Flying</td><td>☐ Throwing Fire</td></tr>
<tr><td>☐ Changing appearance</td><td>☐ Shooting Ice</td></tr>
<tr><td>☐ Controlling metal</td><td>☐ Running Fast</td></tr>
<tr><td>☐ Reading minds</td><td>☐ Teleporting</td></tr>
</table>

Lesson 3: Like Superman

Warm up: Who would win in a fight, Santa Claus or Superman?

Vocabulary

actually	boxing	dancer
guy	ballet	comparable
beard	choreography	opposite

Listening Comprehension 

Watch First: As you watch the video, listen and try to get the main ideas.

- What similarities does the speaker say about Santa Claus and Superman?
- Which similarity is incorrect?
- What are the differences that the speaker mentions about Boxing and Ballet?

Listen for Details: Now listen again and fill in the blanks with vocabulary words as you listen.

I think Superman and Santa Claus are _________________ the same guy, and I'll tell you why: Both fly, both wear red and both have a _________________.

- Do you agree with the speaker's idea?
- What are some differences between Santa Claus and Superman?

To me, boxing is like a ballet, **except** there's no music, no _________________ and the dancers _________________ each other.

- In what ways are boxing and ballet actually similar?
- What are some other differences between ballet and boxing?
- Do you think people would like these jokes in your culture?

Grammar Focus
1. Phrases for Comparison
- ✓ **Use adverbs "quite" or "very" to strengthen the similarity**
- ✓ **Use adverbs "a bit", "a little", "not very" to make it weaker**

Phrase	Similarity	Examples
Equal (adj) The same (adj)	Very high	Everyone has an **equal** chance to win a prize. The UK and Britain are **the same** country. Bob has **the same** hair color **as** Robyn.
Alike (adj) Similar to (adj) Comparable (adj)	Fairly high	John and Jeremy **look** <u>a little</u> **alike** but their height is different. This cookie is <u>very</u> **similar to** my grandmother's homemade cookies. His music is <u>a bit</u> **comparable to** Mozart but not as good.
Be/look/seem/taste/ smell/feel + like	Fairly high	Mungbean soup **smells like** feet but the taste is excellent. My head **feels like** a bomb about to explode.
Different from (adj) The opposite of (adj)	Not similar	Star Wars is <u>quite</u> **different from** Star Trek. White is **the opposite of** black.

Practice: Choose a family member that you are similar or different from and fill out the Venn Diagram. In pairs, explain your diagram to your classmate using the expressions.

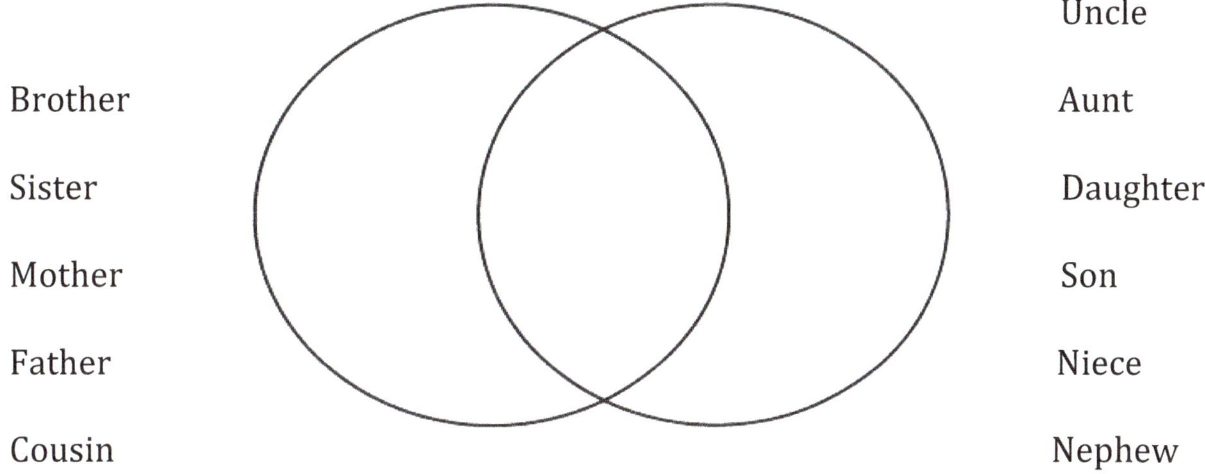

Practice: Choose two countries and fill out the Venn Diagram. In pairs, explain your diagram to your classmate using the expressions.

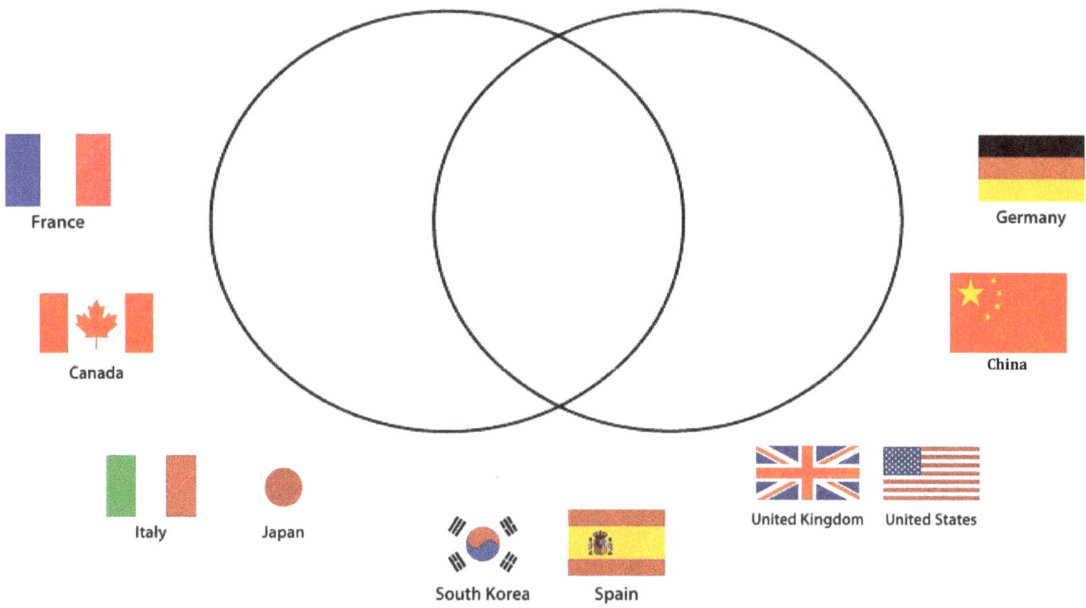

2. Except/Except for
"Except" is another way to say "not including"

Rule	Example
"Except for" is usually used with words of amount like "all", "every", "no", "anybody", "a few", etc.	I ate *everything* **except for** the pickles. The report was perfect **except for** *a few* spelling mistakes.
It can be used as a preposition followed by a noun	I didn't tell *anyone* the secret **except for** <u>Peter</u>. I like your style today **except** <u>the ugly hat</u>.
It can be used as a conjunction followed by a clause.	I would like to help you, **except** <u>I don't have money</u>. I will plan the trip, **except** <u>I won't reserve train tickets yet</u>.
It can be used as a conjunction before "that", "if" and "when"	She doesn't know anything about him **except that** he is rich. She is very beautiful, **except when** she is angry. It is okay to smoke here, **except if** the manager sees you.

Practice: Try to make sentences using "except/except for" with these images.

Discussion Topics:

1. Is there any exception for smoking indoor?

2. Who should be allowed to have guns?

3. What is similar or different between being with friends or being with family?

Lesson 4: Risk Taking

Warm up: Do you like to take risks? What risks have you taken?

Vocabulary:

daredevil	dictates	(for the) thrill
wreck	groceries	eject
tutorial	blinking	crush (noun)
(take a) risk	tank (of gas)	toss
risk-taker	manual	tapping

Listening Comprehension

https://www.oneworldkorea.com/mc---beginner---session-1.html

Watch first: As you watch the video, listen and try to get the main ideas.

- Are the risks in the video big or small?
- Are any of the risks dangerous?

Listen for Details: Now listen again and fill in the blanks with vocabulary words as you listen.

You may not _________________ cars or jump out of buildings, but let's not pretend you don't _________________. You are an everyday _________________.

You sometimes forget to set an alarm, but you wake up anyway. You brush your teeth and then drink orange juice. You drive on an empty _________________ of gas. While other men live their lives as society _________________, you start puzzles from the center. When you drop ice, you kick it under the fridge, you maverick.

You skip _________________. You eat after 9pm. And you check your facebook during work for the _____________. You get in the front seat of taxis and cook chicken that's been in the fridge for four days.

All of your passwords are the same, you _________________. And they don't contain numbers and letters. You wear white and eat spaghetti. You *ARE* the volunteer. And you ask for the recommendation.

When something needs to be thrown away, you _________________ it like Jordan in the fourth quarter. You don't let a _________________ hand tell you when to stop. Electrical plugs? From the cord. You'll open that without even _________________ the top.

You don't _________________. You won't spill. And you'll do all those _________________ in one trip. You guess at names. And when you have a _________________ at work, you always . . .

Hey, I was wondering if you uh. . . uhm. . . maybe you wanna . . . go. . . uh, over to the conference room? We have a meeting . . .

Okay. . .Yeah. ..

Um, okay. Great. . . O-kay bye.

You'll get 'em next time daredevil. Onwards!

<u>**Grammar Focus**</u>

1. Adverbs are used to describe how often you do an action.

Adverb	Frequency	Question	Example
Always	100%	When do you *usually* **sleep**?	I *always* **sleep before 11 pm.**
Usually	90%	Do you *always* **drive** to work?	I *usually* **drive to work.**
Often	60-80%	When do you *usually* **watch** TV?	I *often* **watch TV in the evening.**
Sometimes	50%	Do you *often* **drink** alcohol?	I *sometimes* **drink alcohol.**
Occasionally	30%	Do you *sometimes* **diet**?	I *occasionally* **go on a diet.**
Rarely	10%	How *often* **do** you **read**?	I *rarely* **read the newspaper.**
Never	0%	Do you *usually* **swim**?	I *never* **swim in the ocean.**

Practice 1: In pairs, ask and answer the questions using an adverb of frequency

1) How often do you brush your teeth? Where do you _____________ brush them?

2) What time do you wake up? Are you ___________ tired?

3) What time do you start work? Are you _____________ on-time?

4) When do you eat dinner? Do you _____________cook, get delivery, or eat out?

5) When do you take vacation? Do you _____________ go to the same place?

6) How many hours do you sleep? Do you _____________ sleep well?

7) How often do you go shopping? What do you _____________ buy?

8) When do you relax? Where do you _____________ like to go?

9) When do you meet your friends? Where do you _____________ meet them?

2. More Adverb Rules

Rule:	Example:
The adverb usually comes after the verb "be"	I always am late → I am always late I sometimes am tired → I am sometimes tired He usually isn't sad → He isn't usually sad
The adverb can go between two verbs (Can/Should/Need to / have to / try to, etc.)	I *sometimes* **can sing** well - OR - I **can** *sometimes* **sing** well She *usually* **doesn't wash** the dishes - OR - She **doesn't** *usually* **wash** the dishes.

<u>Practice 2:</u> Put the following sentences into the correct order.

1) runs / everyday / he / usually   _______________________________________

2) They / movies / always / talk about _______________________________________

3) I / a big / eater / am / sometimes _______________________________________

4) never / I / the gym / go to   _______________________________________

5) drink / occasionally / they / milk _______________________________________

6) drink / need to / often / water / You _______________________________________

7) her secrets / tells / rarely / to anyone / she _______________________________________

8) after / tired / work / often / They / are _______________________________________

9) I / understand / can / sometimes _______________________________________

<u>Discussion:</u> In pairs or small groups practice making questions with these situations. Then answer the questions using frequency adverbs.

Leave your umbrella at home when it rains

Drive over the speed limit

Go to the doctor

Not read the manual before doing something

Check SNS during work hours

Turn off your alarm and sleep again

Forget someone's name

Change your password

Volunteer to do something

Eat old food

Lesson 5: The Homer Diet

Warm up: "Assal horizontology" (humorous word): The act of sitting around doing nothing for long periods of time.

- How often do you practice "assal horizontology"?

- How often do you eat unhealthy food?

Vocabulary

Available	Process	Creative
Dangerously	Neglected	Instead of
Underweight	Whipped Cream	Chew
Individual	Congealed	Brush teeth
Recommend	Fantastic	Rub
Gorging	Speed up	Window

Listening Comprehension 

https://www.oneworldkorea.com/mc---beginner---session-1.html

Watch first: As you watch the video, listen and try to get the main ideas.

- What kind of diet is Dr. Nick recommending?

- What are three ways to do this diet?

- How can Homer see if the food is unhealthy?

Listen for Details: Now listen again and fill in the blanks with vocabulary words as you listen.

Dr. Nick: Hi everybody!
Bart & Homer: Hi Doctor Nick!
Dr. Nick: Now there are many options available for dangerously _______________ individuals like yourself. I recommend a slow steady ______________ process, combined with "assal horizontology."

- What problem does Dr. Nick think that Homer has? What cure is he recommending?

Homer: Of course!
Dr. Nick: You will want to focus on the ________________ food groups, such as the whipped group, the congealed group, and the "chocola-tastic".
Homer: What can I do to ______________ the whole thing ___________ doctor?
Dr. Nick: Well, be _________________. Instead of making sandwiches with bread, use pop-tarts. Instead of chewing gum, chew bacon.

- What kind of food groups is Dr. Nick recommending? Do you think Dr. Nick is a good doctor?

Bart: You could ______________ your _______________ with milkshakes!

Dr. Nick: Hey, did you go to Hollywood Upstairs Medical College too? ... And remember, if you are not sure about something, _________________ it against a piece of paper. If the paper turns clear, it's your ____________________ to weight gain. Bye, bye everybody!

- Do you think Hollywood Upstairs Medical College is a good medical school?

Grammar Focus

1. Modals of Recommendation
Use the following modals to make recommendations by pairing them with a base verb.

Modal	Strength	Example
must/have to	100%	You *must* <u>sleep</u> at least 5 hours every night.
had better	90%	You *had better* <u>take</u> medicine.
should	80%	You *should* <u>wash</u> your hands more often.
could/might	50%	You *could* <u>try</u> a yoga class.
shouldn't	- 80%	You *shouldn't* <u>drink</u> so much alcohol.
had better not	- 90%	You *had better not* <u>smoke</u> cigarettes.
must not	- 100%	You *must not* <u>eat</u> junk food.

Practice: In pairs, ask the following questions and answer by using a modal of recommendation. Then asking some follow up questions.

- *I want to lose weight. What type of diet or exercise should I do?*
    - Example follow up questions:
        - What types of food do you like to eat?
        - Do you like to play any sports?
        - How often do you exercise?

- *I want to take a vacation abroad. Where should I go?*
    - Example follow up questions:
        - How much time do you have?
        - How much money can you spend?
        - Who will you travel with?
        - What type of activities do you want to do?

2. Using "Instead of"

Structure: **Instead of** <u>verb+ing</u> (object), <u>verb</u> (object)

Example: **Instead of** <u>eating</u> junk food, <u>eat</u> fresh vegetables.

Example: **Instead of** <u>watching</u> TV, <u>go</u> to the gym.

Practice: Choose which ending of the sentence you agree with more and then discuss with your partner why you agree or disagree with this advice.

1. Instead of spending a lot of money on your wedding, ____________________

   ☐ Spend more on your honeymoon **OR** ☐ Buy a bigger house

   ☐ Invest in stocks **OR** ☐ Buy nicer wedding rings

2. Instead of starting your career right after graduation, ____________________

   ☐ Travel the world with a backpack **OR** ☐ Start a your own business

   ☐ Live with your parents and relax **OR** ☐ Live abroad for a year

Conversation Practice

Read the conversation example, then try to make your own similar conversation using the problems listed or add your own.

Patient: Doctor, I have a problem. I often <u>get backaches.</u>

Doctor: I recommend <u>taking pain medicine</u>, combined with frequent <u>yoga exercise</u>.

Patient: What can I do to speed my recovery up?

Doctor: Well, instead of <u>staying at your desk all the time, get up and walk around.</u> Instead of <u>carrying heavy things, tell your husband to carry them</u>.

Patient: Okay, thanks doc. I'll try that!

Patient: Doctor, I have a problem. I often ________________.

Doctor: I recommend ______________, combined with frequent ________________.

Patient: What can I do to speed my health condition up?

Doctor: ....

Patient: ....

Ideas for Health Problems
Drink too much alcohol
Can't sleep at night
Get stomachaches
Get headaches
Have allergies
Have red eyes
Have a skin rash

Lesson 6: Job Experience

Warm up: Choose 2 or 3 accomplishments you did in the past.
When did you accomplish this? How did you feel about this experience?

- ☐ Graduated
- ☐ Won an award
- ☐ Moved to a new city
- ☐ Learned another language

- ☐ Did an extreme sport
- ☐ Got a job
- ☐ Got married
- ☐ Traveled
- ☐ Played an instrument

- ☐ Bought a car
- ☐ Ran a marathon
- ☐ Volunteered
- ☐ Raised children

Vocabulary:

Pull up	Manager	Responsibility
Smile/Smiley	Counter	Fit in
Fill out	Possible	Experience
Application	Amount	

Listening Comprehension

https://www.oneworldkorea.com/mc---beginner---session-1.html

Watch first: As you watch the video, listen and try to get the main ideas.

- What does Lester order and how much does it cost?
- Why does Lester want to apply for a job at Mister Smiley's?
- Why are the clerk and manager surprised that Lester is applying?

Listen for Details

Now listen again and fill in the blanks with vocabulary words as you listen.

Lester: I'd like the Big Barn Burger, Smiley Fries and an ______________ _________________.

Clerk: Please pull up to the window. Thank you! Smile you are at Mister Smiley's that will be four-ninety-eight please.   Would you like some smiley sauce?

Lester: No, actually, I'd like to fill out an _________________________.

Clerk: There're no jobs for _________________. It's only counter.

Lester: Good. *I'm looking* for the least possible amount of ____________________.

Manager: I don't think you'd fit in here.

Lester: I have ________________ _________________ experience.

Manager: Yeah, like ___________________ years ago.

- Did you ever have a part time job?
- What are the positives and negatives of working at a fast food restaurant?

Grammar Focus:

Present Continuous

Used to describe: 1) actions happening now   2) general actions happening in the future

(SUBJECT)	BE	V + ING **[NOW]**	V+ING **[FUTURE]**
I	am	calling my mom	calling my mom *tomorrow*
He / She / It	Is	planning the meeting	planning the meeting *next week*
We / You / They	are	traveling together	traveling together *this summer*

Practice 1: In pairs, ask and answer questions about the people in the photos.

Example: What **are** they **doing**? ➔   They **are practicing** a dance.
When **are** they **performing**?   They**'re performing** <u>tomorrow</u>.

Practice 2: Look at the scenes below. In pairs, take turns describing what you see in each scene using present continuous. Be creative!

He is...

She is...

They are....

The chocolate is...

He is...

She is...

The people are....

The bus is...

Conversation: Discuss the following questions using present continuous and free talking. Remember details about what you partner says so you can share them with the whole class.

Don't forget to continue the conversation using your WH- Questions.
(Why, What, When, Where, How [long, many, much])

What is happening now?

Where are you working now?

What are you doing now at work?

What is your family doing now?

Are you helping your parents with anything?

Are you saving money for anything nowadays?

Are you trying any new hobbies?

Are you getting enough sleep?

____

____

____

____

____

____

What is happening in the future?

When are you planning to retire?

Where are you traveling for your next vacation?

Who are you planning to speak English with?

Are you planning to buy anything new?

When are you waking up tomorrow morning?

When are you going to bed tomorrow?

What are you doing this weekend?

Lesson 7: Surprises

Warm up: Do you like planned events or surprises? What is a surprise you've experienced?

- ✓ Birthday Party
- ✓ Test Results
- ✓ Marriage/Engagement

- ✓ Baby
- ✓ April Fool's Day
- ✓ Electricity Bill

Vocabulary

Note	Take/took	Feed/Fed
Decision	Give/gave	Raise/Raised
Radish	Deliver/delivered	

Listening Comprehension  https://www.oneworldkorea.com/mc---beginner---session-1.html

Watch first: As you watch the video, listen and try to get the main ideas.

- Where did Mr. Ping find Po? What was Po doing?

- What did he do to the lost panda?

- What decision did he make?

Listen for Details: Now listen again and fill in the blanks with vocabulary words as you listen.

Po: How did I get here, Dad? Where did I come from?

Mr. Ping: Actually, you came from this. It was just another day at the restaurant. Time to make the noodles. I went out to the back, where my vegetables had just been __________. There were cabbages, turnips, __________. Only, there were no ________, just a very hungry baby panda. There was no _______. Of course, you could have eaten it. I waited for someone to come looking for you, but no one did.

> - Have you ever found something unexpected? (EX: money on the ground, seeing an old friend, meeting a celebrity, etc)

I brought you inside, ________ you, _______ you a bath, and ______ you again, and again, and tried to put some pants on you. And then I made a ________ that changed my life forever. To make my soup without radishes, and to __________ you as my own son.

> - Do you raise a pet or child? Is it easy or difficult?

> - What is the most valuable or important thing you lost? Did you get it back?

Grammar Focus

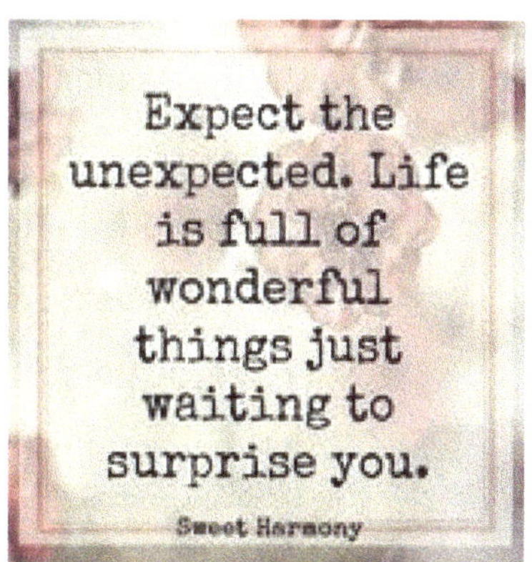

1. Simple Past

✓ Used to talk about past stories and experiences

Positive: Subject + Past Verb	I **jogged** at the park.
Negative: Subject + Did Not + Base Verb	I **didn't walk** my dog. It rained.
Yes/No Question: Did +Subject + Base Verb?	**Did** you **go** to the convenience store? [Yes, I did.] **Did** he **work** on the project yet? [No, he didn't.]
WH-Questions: [WH] + Did + Subject + Base Verb?	**Where did** they **eat** last night? [At the Thai restaurant.] **When did** we **start** the meeting? [At 9:00. You're late.] **Who did** you **meet** this weekend? [Just my friend.]

Practice 1: Ask your partner about their week with different times. Be ready to share your partner's past activities with the class.

What did you do ....?
- ✓ Yesterday? ______________________________
- ✓ Last Weekend? ______________________________
- ✓ On Monday? ______________________________
- ✓ Last Friday? ______________________________
- ✓ This morning? ______________________________
- ✓ At 8:00pm, two days ago? ______________________________

Practice 2: Use the chart to play tic-tac-toe with a partner. One person is O and the other is X. The person asking the question writes their O or X in a square and other student should answer the question. Whoever gets three in a row is the winner. The answer doesn't have to be true.

Example Questions:	**Example Answers:**
<u>What</u> did you **read** last?	I **read** the newspaper this morning.
When did you **eat** dinner yesterday?	I **ate** dinner at 7:30pm last night.
Where did you **play** soccer on Saturday?	I **played** soccer at Central Park on Saturday.

Tic-Tac-Toe Question and Answer Game

	study	eat	listen [Music]	cook	sing	cry	wake up	play [SPORT]
What								
Where								
When								

Story telling

With you partner share stories about your past experiences considering the topics below. When your partner is telling a story make sure to ask questions to get more details.

Topics:

- ✓ A traffic accident
- ✓ A memory of life before smartphones
- ✓ The day you graduated from high school
- ✓ A time you got in an argument
- ✓ A time you got lost
- ✓ An experience with bad weather

Example:

A: I got in a traffic accident last year.   B: What was the accident?

A: As I drove my car, I saw a cat in the road.
   I tried to avoid the cat and crashed!   B: Where did you crash?

A: I hit a parked car.   B: Oh no! Did you get hurt?

A: No, but I had to pay for the damage to the
   Other car.   B: How much did you pay?

A: I had to pay a lot because it was an
   expensive car   B: Did the cat survive?

A: I hope so! That cat cost me a lot of money!

Lesson 8: Worst Hotel Ever

Warm up: Do you often travel for work or pleasure? Where do you usually travel?

Vocabulary

Experience	Ding	Entire
A couple (of)	Outside	For that matter
Vicinity	Loud	PC (politically correct)
Sold out	On the hour	

Listening Comprehension  https://www.oneworldkorea.com/mc---beginner---session-1.html

Watch first: As you watch the video, listen and try to get the main ideas.
- Why did she travel?

- What was the problem at her hotel?

- What happened after the problem?

Listen for Details: Now listen again and fill in the blanks with vocabulary words as you listen.

So I had the worst hotel __________ ever! First off, this was a conference that was about 20,000 people, and all the hotels in the __________ were sold out. So I got lucky to get into this hotel which was a __________ blocks away.

- Have you ever been to a busy/crowded place where many hotels were sold out?

And I went to the conference, the conference was great, went back to the room, was ready to go to sleep. At around 11:00pm, there was this dinging __________, went to the window and I'm like, wow. There's a train outside my window. It was **really really** __________! It kept going over and over and over again. Every hour, __________. 1:00am, 2:00am, 3:00am, 4:00am and it stopped at 5:00am.

- Have you ever slept near a train / construction / loud noise? How long did it last?

So, I ended up getting no sleep the __________ time I was at this conference. And everyone kept telling me how tired I look. Which if you're a woman or anyone ______________, you never liked to be told you're tired because that's really __________ for you look like poo. And that didn't make me feel better.

- Is it okay to tell someone "You look tired!"? Why/why not?

Grammar Focus

Simple Past (Continued)

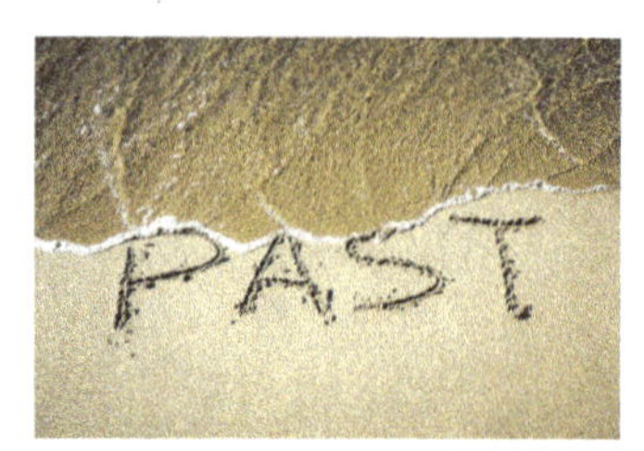

- ✓ Used to talk about past stories and experiences

- ✓ For negative sentences add "didn't" before the base verb.

- ✓ "Did" is used with the base verb to make questions

- ✓ To make be-verbs past tense use "was" or "were"

	Regular	**Irregular** *See page 54 for more examples
Positive	He **walked** all day. (walk) She **danced** with her husband (dance)	They **gave** me a birthday present. (give) I **was** drunk last night. (be)
Negative	They **didn't play** last week. (play) She **didn't watch** the game. (watch)	We **didn't eat** anything. (eat) They **weren't** thieves. (be)
Y/ N Question	**Did** you **solve** the problem? **Did** he **punch** my dog?	**Did** she **learn** Spanish? **Was** she late this morning?
WH-Question	Why **did** she **dump** him? When **did** you **bake** this bread?	Where **did** they **run** yesterday? What **was** his problem?

Practice 1: Use the "Common Traveling Verbs" to ask questions about your partner's last experience.
Use the following structure:

Q: When was the last time you (past tense verb)?

A: The last time I (past tense verb) was (time).

Example:

A: When was the last time you swam?

B: The last time I swam was a year ago.

A: Where did you swim?

B: I swam in the ocean near Pusan.

A: Did you swim with anyone else?

B: Yes, I swam with my daughter.

A: Was the water cold?

B: No it was summer time.

Common Traveling Verbs	
Go	Went
Fly	Flew
Visit	Visited
Leave	Left
Arrive	Arrived
Drive	Drove
Pack	Packed
Ride	Rode
Take	Took
Check in/out	Checked in/out
Reserve	Reserved
Travel	Traveled
Rent	Rented
Stay	Stayed

<u>Practice 2:</u> In pairs, talk about your BEST or WORST vacation experience using simple past. Write down your partner's answers to the following questions, and be ready to retell their story.

1. Where did you go? ____
2. Who did you go with? ____
3. How long did you stay? ____
4. What did you do? ____
5. How was the food? ____
6. How was the weather? ____
7. What did you like/dislike most about the trip? _____________________

Activity – Honeymoon Stories

We will make funny stories about a couple and their honeymoon. Each student will make one sentence to add to the story by choosing a word from the "Common Traveling Verbs" list. Be creative. As a class we will practice one story together, then split into groups to make more stories.

Example:

Student A: The new couple **went** to <u>Malaysia</u> on their honeymoon.

Student B: They **arrived** at their <u>beach hotel</u> and it **was** <u>very dirty</u>.

Student C: Then, they **complained** to <u>the hotel staff</u> and **got** a <u>new room</u>.

Student D: After that, they **swam** and ...

Lesson 9: Crime Witness

Warm up: Do you like watching mystery or crime dramas/movies? Why or why not?

Vocabulary

Landmark	Detective	Catch one's eye
Statue	Culprit	Attractive
Bizarre	Slip the net	Stunning
Berserk	Patrol	Vanish
Questioning	Nun	Pleasure

Listening Comprehension 

Watch first: As you watch the video, listen and try to get the main ideas.

- Why are the police holding the nuns in Saint Paul's Cathedral?
- What did the guard witness last night?
- Why does the guard seem excited to describe the nun's appearance?

Listen for Details

Listen for Details: Now listen again and fill in the blanks with vocabulary words as you listen.

Guide: Designed by Sir Christopher Wren. Saint Paul's Cathedral is one of London's most famous landmarks. Sadly the Great Dome is closed to visitors today as one of its statues was destroyed in a _______________ accident last night. But if you follow me this way...

Mary: Excuse me? What happened here?   **Guard:** A nun went berserk.   **Mary:** Really?

Guard: It happens. The police have rounded them all up for _________________. Hold it there, sister. You're going nowhere until the detective says so. Spin it around. Mind you, if you ask me, the real culprit _____________ __________ _____________.

Jonathan: What makes you say that?

Guard: Because I saw her. That's what. I _was_ on patrol in the upper dome _watching_ the nuns parade far below _when_ something ____________ _________ _____________. One of them broke free from the herd, made her way to the Whispering Gallery. Only the good Lord knows what she _was doing_ up there. But she was never going to get away with it. Not _while_ I'm Vice Deputy Head of Security.

Guard: Oye! Attention all units. An unusually _________________ nun is causing mayhem in the cathedral dome. Activate emergency protocol. Stop that stunning sister. I set off at lightning speed but by the time we'd locked the place down, she'd vanished into the night... Most beautiful woman I've seen in a long time.

Mary: Do you think you might be able to describe her?

Guard: It would be my _________________.

- Do you like to visit historical sites and museums? How often do you visit them?
- Do you think the guard's story is accurate? Why or why not?

Grammar Focus

Past Continuous

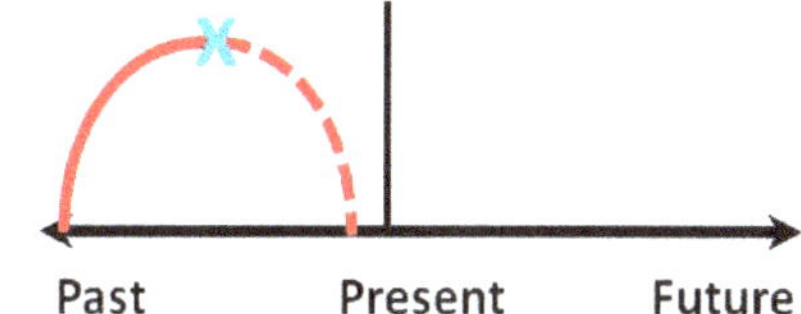

- ✓ Use the past continuous for a longer action in the past that was interrupted.
- ✓ The interruption is usually a shorter action in simple past.

[WH-Q] + **WAS/WERE** + subject+ verb/ing	subject + **WAS/WERE** + verb+ing + time
Was she studying *when I called?*	Yes, she was studying *when you called.*
What **were** you doing *when the earthquake started?*	I **was** watching TV *when the earthquake started.*
Where **were** you driving *yesterday at 6pm?*	We **were** driving to the theater *yesterday at 6pm.*
Why **was** he sleeping *at noon?*	He **was** sleeping *at noon* because he was tired.

- ✓ You can also use a specific time as the interruption

Practice: Chain Game
In a group, practice making past continuous questions and sentences with the times below. Make note of the answer to the questions.

Example: What were you doing at 10pm yesterday?
    A: I **was** finishing work at 10pm yesterday.   **B:** I **was** eating dinner.   **C:** I **was** walking my dog.

- Sunday at 3pm   ____

- Yesterday at 9pm   ____

- Today at 7am   ____

- Friday at 10pm   ____

- Tuesday at noon   ____

- Saturday at 11am   ____

- Wednesday at 10am   ____

After practicing the basic sentences, now create a chain. The first student repeats the basic sentence with time. The second student continues the sentence using *'When the first student was verb+ing'*. The third student continues from the second, and so on.

Example: A: I **was** finishing work at 10pm yesterday.

    B: *When he was working*, I **was** eating dinner.

    C: *When he was working and she was eating*, I **was** walking my dog.

Discussion
Talk about an accident experienced by you, a friend, a family member, or a coworker using the past continuous and simple past. Ask WH Questions to get detailed information.

Hit by falling object

Got burned

Be shocked by electric

Set on fire

Stubbed a toe

Tripped and fell

Slipped and fell

Role Play – Lost and Found

You've lost something valuable. You are talking to a security officer at the lost-and-found. Explain your lost item in detail. Use the example dialogue as a guide:

Locations: Subway Department store Elevator Restaurant

Salon Movie Theater Bus

Example:

A: Hello, excuse me. Can you help me? I lost my ______.

B: Sure, where did you lose your ______?

A: Well, I was …

B: Can you describe what it looks like?

A: It is …

B: …

A: Please call me when you find it. My number is …

Remember to...

- ✓ Give a lot of details, which describe the lost item.
- ✓ Explain how important this item is for you.
- ✓ Ask questions about how it can be found.

Lesson 10: Nightmare Interview

Warm up: Are you good or bad at interviews?

What was your best or worst interview experience?

Vocabulary:

Interview	Nervous	Sense of (fashion, taste. .)
Qualified	Graduate	Glamorous
Candidate	Human Resources	Skinny
Assistant	Hear of (sth)	Fit
Journalist	Smart	Confident

Listening Comprehension  https://www.oneworldkorea.com/mc---beginner---session-1.html

Watch first: As you watch the video, listen and try to get the main ideas.

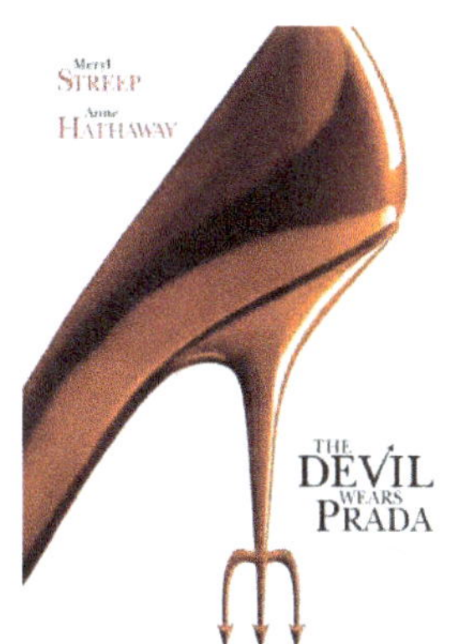

- Is this a good or bad interview?

- What job do you think Andy is applying for?

- Is Andy qualified?

Listen for Details

Now listen again and fill in the blanks with vocabulary words as you listen.

Miranda: Who are you?

Andy: Uh, my name is Andy Sachs. I recently _______________ from Northwestern University.

Miranda: And what are you doing here?[Clears Throat]

Andy: Well, I think I could do a good job as your _______________. And, um… Yeah, I came to New York to be a _______________ and sent letters out everywhere… and then finally got a call from Elias-Clarke… and met with Sherry up at Human _______________. Basically, it's this or Auto Universe.

Miranda: So you don't read Runway ?

Andy: Uh, no.

Miranda: And before today, you had never heard of me.

Andy: No.

Miranda: And you <u>have no style</u> or sense of _______________.

Andy: Well, um. I think that depends on what you're-

Miranda: No, no. That wasn't a question.

Andy: Um, I was editor in chief of the Daily Northwesternern. I also, um, won a national _______________ for college journalists… with my series on the janitors' union, which exposed the exploitation –

Miranda: That's all.

- What mistakes did Andy make in preparing for this interview?

- What do you think is most important in an interview?
  - ☐ Appearance   ☐ Education
  - ☐ Personality   ☐ Experience
  - ☐ Knowing the company

Grammar Focus:

HAVE vs. IS

- ✓ Both can be used to Describe something
- ✓ Have/Has is followed by nouns, Is/Are is followed by adjectives

Have / Has + NOUN	Is / Are + ADJECTIVE
She **has** dark hair.	Her hair **is** dark.
He **has** great talent!	His talent **is** great!
They **don't have** old clothes.	Their clothes **are** new.
Do they **have** intelligence?	**Are** they smart?
Doesn't she **have** any fat?	**Isn't** she skinny?

Practice 1: Fill in the blank with the correct use of " have / doesn't have / is / isn't"

1) The building _________________ a lot of floors
2) His smile ________________ friendly.
3) The project ________________ failing.
4) The dress ________________ nice colors.
5) Those movies ______________ the same director.
6) The students ______________ any time.

Practice 2: Based on the video, describe the characters personality and appearance.

Example:
Andy is not glamorous.
Andy has a degree from Northwestern University.

Consider some of these questions:

What is she wearing?

What is her physical appearance?

How does she feel at the interview?

What is her personality?

<u>Practice 3</u>: With a partner, describe the following people making one sentence with "is + adjective" and one sentence with "have + noun".

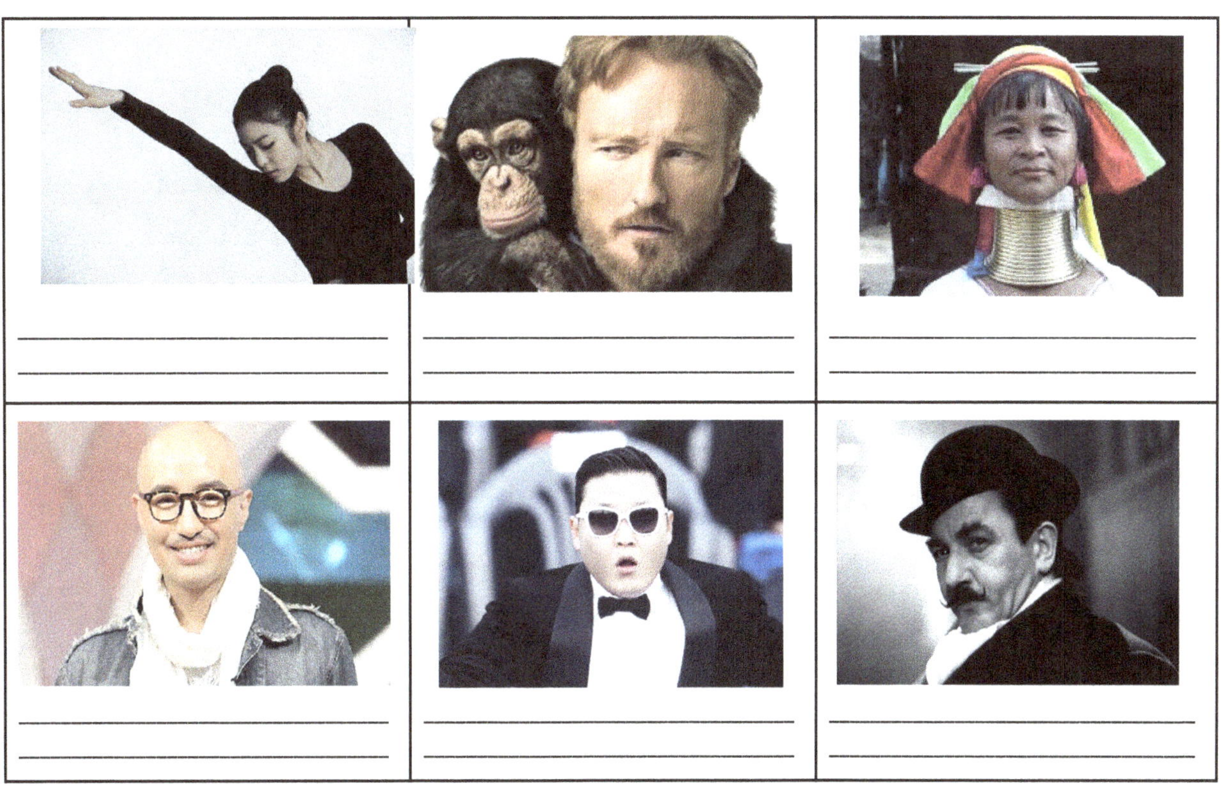

<u>Conversation:</u>

In pairs, discuss the following questions. Take notes on your partners opinions and be ready to summarize your partners ideas with the whole class.

1. Which personality traits do you think are most important to have?
   ✓ For a person applying at your company
   ✓ For a friend
   ✓ For a politician
   ✓ For you boss/manager

Funny	Active	Smart
Serious	Honest	Reliable
Calm	Polite	Creative
Diligent	Patient	Generous
Brave	Energetic	Other: ________________

1. Who is your favorite celebrity? Describe the things you like about them.

2. Who are you more similar to, your mom or your dad? How?

Lesson 11: Home Basics

Warm up: What is your favorite place to relax? Why?

Vocabulary:

Nightstand	Chester drawers	Curtain
Alarm	Futon	Bookcase
Pro-athlete	(bed) frame	Twin / King / Queen size
Heinous	Furniture	Garage
Ingredient	Mattress	Cabinet

Listening Comprehension  https://www.oneworldkorea.com/mc---beginner---session-2.html

Watch first: As you watch the video, listen and try to get the main ideas.

- How many items does Leigh Anne talk about?

- What kind of room is she describing?

- Does Michael like his new room?

Listen for Details: Now listen again and fill in the blanks with vocabulary words as you listen.

Leigh Anne: Over here, you have a desk, chester _______. You have a ________, a light, an ______.
Oh, and Shawn says all the pro-_____ use _____ if they can't find a bed big enough, so I got you
one of those. Of course the ______ was heinous. I was not about to let that in my house, but I got
you something nicer.

Michael: It's mine?

Leigh Anne: Yes, sir. . . . .What? Never had one before? What? A room to yourself?

Michael: A bed.

Leigh Anne: Well, you have one now.

- What is something you never had but have always wanted?

Grammar Focus

Countable & Uncountable Nouns

- ✓ A **countable noun** is an object you can separate and count individually (ex. apple)

- ✓ In singular form, countable nouns use "a / an / the" (ex. **the** apple)

- ✓ In plural form, most countable nouns add an "s" to the end (ex. apple**s**)

- ✓ An **uncountable noun** is an object you cannot separate and count individually (ex. water)

- ✓ They need containers to count them (ex. **a glass of** water)

Countable noun	Plural Form		Containers to count	Uncountable noun	Plural Form
Regular:	**Regular:**		a **piece** of	Furniture	
a chair	chairs		a **bowl** of	Fruit	
a bed	beds		a **tube** of	Toothpaste	
a window	windows		a **bag** of	Money	
an event	events		a **jar** of	Salt	
a mattress	mattresses		a **barrel** of	Oil	None
			a **can** of	Soup	
Irregular:	**Irregular:**		a **breath** of	Air	
Child	Children		a **bar** of	Soap	
Person	People		a **slice** of	Pie	
Woman	Women		a **carton** of	Milk	
Foot	Feet		a **cup / glass** of	Water	
Fish	Fish		a **pound / liter /**	Cola	
Tooth	Teeth		**kilogram** of	Meat	

Practice 1: Work with a partner. Partner A will look at the images below and Parter B will look at the images on the next page. Using "There is/are" each partner should describe what is in their image and find how they are similar and different. Make sure to use containers for uncountable nouns.

    Example: Partner A: "There is a carton of milk on the table"

        Partner B: "Is there a glass of water on the table too?"

        Partner A: "No, there isn't a glass of water."

<u>Partner A Image:</u>

Example: Partner A: "There is a carton of milk on the table"

Partner B: "Is there a glass of water on the table too?"

Partner A: "No, there isn't a glass of water."

Discussion:

Talk about your housing preferences using the "would you rather". When possible, try using adjectives like *big, wide, small, beautiful, clean* and adverbs like *any, much, many,* and *a lot of.* Use this question structure:

When you choose a place to live, would you rather have ____________ or ____________?

Example: Would you rather have *many* <u>rooms</u> or *a big* <u>kitchen</u>?

Terrace	vs	Rooftop
Swimming Pool	vs	Garden
Bookshelves	vs	TV screen
Ground floor	vs	Top floor
Windows	vs	Air conditioning
Countryside	vs	City center
Wood floor	vs	Carpet
Privacy	vs	Silence
Chef	vs	Maid service

Lesson 12: Making & Breaking Plans

Warm up: Is there someone who you don't like to spend time with? Do you avoid that person?

Vocabulary

forget	show someone around	close
place	bummer	attend
booze	peacefully	gentle
yourself	visit	neutral
move	far away	firm
in town	a drive	

Listening Comprehension (0:00 – 1:15)  https://www.oneworldkorea.com/mc---beginner---session-2.html

Watch first: As you watch the video, listen and try to get the main ideas.

- What is Zach inviting everyone to and where?

- What are the reasons that each of his friends can't go?

- Why is everyone surprised about Quinta's answer?

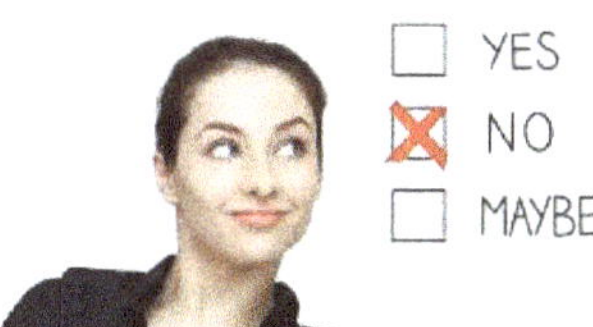

Listen for Details: Now listen again and fill in the blanks with vocabulary words as you listen.

Steve: I mean Zach, you put the "power" in PowerPoint today.
Zach: Right, yeah for sure. Hey guys, don't forget. A party this weekend at ________
______________. Bring booze, chips, and most importantly __________________.
Steve: Oh, I can't make it on Friday. I agreed to help a friend ______________ and I don't know what time we're going to be done.

- Do you think Steve is telling the truth? How often do you help your friends move?

Kyle: Yeah, I wish I could go too but my dad is _________ ______________. I've got to show him around the old city. You know how dads are.
Steve: Dad's love cities.
Zach: Well _________________, umm... well what about you Quinta?
Quinta: I can't go either **because** I don't want to.
Zach: Um, what, I'm sorry? Do you have something to do?
Quinta: Uh no. I, um, I just don't want to go.

- Do you think it is rude for Quinta to say this? Should she make a fake excuse?

Kyle: Huh... Do you uh... Is your dad in town? Do you have to take him around the city too?
Quinta: Oh, no, no, no. My dad is living ________________ in Philadelphia. He hasn't visited in years. I just don't want to go.
Steve: You don't want to go because it's ___________ ____________. **Because** it's in Studio City and that's a drive.
Quinta: Actually, I live pretty _______________ to Studio City, in the Valley. Yeah, I just don't want to attend the party.

- If you were Zach, would you be angry at Quinta?

Grammar Focus

1. Using "Because"

Use "because" before the reason in a sentence	*I can't go to the party* **because** I <u>am</u> sick. I <u>need to</u> walk my dog. I <u>have to</u> work late. I <u>want to</u> see a movie instead. I <u>don't like</u> your sister.
Put the "because" clause at the beginning of the sentence to stress the reason more	**Because** it <u>is</u> snowing outside, *she will be late.* **Because** she <u>needs to</u> buy a gift, **Because** she <u>has to</u> meet a fiend, **Because** she <u>wants to</u> buy coffee, **Because** she <u>likes</u> to come late,
The result clause isn't necessary when answering a question	*Why aren't they eating?* **Because** they <u>are</u> not hungry. **Because** they <u>need to</u> lose weight. **Because** they <u>have to</u> eat healthy. **Because** they <u>want to</u> eat later. **Because** they <u>don't like</u> this food.
In casual speaking, native speakers sometimes shorten "because" to "cuz"	*Winter sucks* **cuz** it<u>'s</u> too cold. **cuz** I <u>need</u> more sunshine. **cuz** I <u>have to</u> wear a jacket all the time. **cuz** I <u>want to</u> swim outside. **cuz** I <u>like</u> wearing shorts.

<u>Practice 1:</u> In pairs add reasons to the opinions below by using "because".

1. I like/don't like the president...
2. I like/don't like my boss...
3. ______________ is the best season in my country...
4. I need a pay raise...
5. My favorite movie is ______________...
6. Some people get married in their thirties...
7. Some people in my country attend university...
8. You should not eat fried chicken every day...

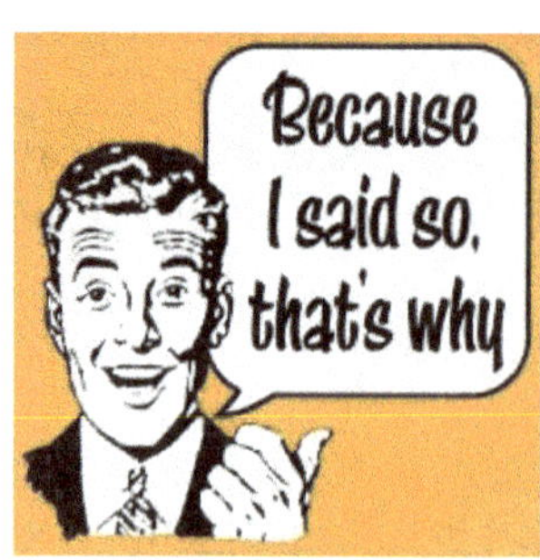

2. Saying no politely.

Gentle	Neutral	Firm

I wish I could but...
     I have to do homework.
 I'm sorry but...
     I am too busy.
	I'll take a rain check.
	     I have to do homework.
	 I can't because...
	     I am too busy.
		No thanks.
		     I have to do homework.
		 No, I'm not going to because...
		     I am too busy.

<u>Practice 2:</u> In pairs ask the following questions and use the phrases to say no in different ways.

1. Can you come to my party this weekend?
2. Do you want to go on a date with my coworker?
3. Would you like to join me for coffee?
4. Can you help me move my apartment on Friday night?
5. Will you let me use your car for my vacation?
6. Do you want to drink 10 cans of energy drink with me tonight?
7. Would you like to see a horror movie with me?
8. Would you like to pay for my dinner tonight?

Conversation Practice

Read the conversation example, then in pairs try to make your own similar conversation.

Zach: Hey, Steve let's <u>get coffee together</u> some time.

Steve: Okay, that sounds great. When are you available?

Zach: How about tonight?

Steve: Oh, I'm sorry but <u>tonight I have yoga class.</u> How about tomorrow?

Zach: I wish I could but <u>I need to work late</u> tomorrow.

Steve: Are you free this weekend?

Zach: No, I can't this weekend because <u>I am hiking Mount Everest</u>.

Steve: Okay then, I'll take a rain check.

Zach: Yeah, let's plan to <u>get coffee together </u>another time.

Steve: Alright, <u>see you later</u>!

A: Hey, Steve let's ______________________________ some time.

B: Yeah, that sounds great. When are you available?

A: How about tonight?

B: Oh, I'm sorry but ____________________________. How about tomorrow?

A: I wish I could but ____________________________tomorrow.

B: Are you free this weekend?

A: No, I can't this weekend because ____________________________.

B: Okay then, I'll take a rain check.

A: Yeah, let's plan to ______________________________ another time.

B: Alright, ________________________________!

Lesson 13: Party Pooper

Warm up: Do you enjoy attending social events? Which of the following do you like or dislike?

☐ Wedding   ☐ Holiday gathering   ☐ Company dinner
☐ Housewarming party   ☐ Birthday party   ☐ Baby's first birthday

Vocabulary

Unbelievable	Warn	Survival
Projecting	Camouflaged	Bunker
Ruin	Fortified	Party Pooper

Listening Comprehension

https://www.oneworldkorea.com/mc---beginner---session-2.html

Watch first: As you watch the video, listen and try to get the main ideas.

- Why is Branch complaining about Poppy and her friends?

- Why do the other Trolls think that Branch is a party pooper?

Listen for Details: Now listen again and fill in the blanks with vocabulary words as you listen.

Branch: Unbelievable guys, really, really, great good job. I could hear you from a mile away.

Poppy: Good I was worried we weren't _______________________ enough.

Branch: Poppy, if I can hear you so can the Bergens.

Other Trolls: Oh boy. Here we go again. Oh Branch! You always ____________________ everything, warning us about the Bergens.

Branch: No I don't... The Bergens are coming! Ah! The Bergens are coming! Ah! The Bergens are coming! Ah!

Poppy: Come on. We haven't seen a Bergen in 20 years, they're not going to find us.

Branch: No they're not going to find me because I'll be in my highly camouflaged, heavily fortified Bergen-proof ____________________ ___________________.

Poppy: You mean you're not coming to the party tonight?

Other Trolls: But it's going to be _the biggest, the loudest, the craziest party ever!_

Branch: Big, loud, crazy? You're just going to lead the Bergens right to us.

Other Trolls: Are you sure you want to invite this ________________ __________________ to poop on your party?

- Do you know anyone who is a party pooper like Branch?

- How often do you host parties? Do you enjoy being a party host?

Grammar Focus

1. Superlative
- ✓ Adjectives with one syllable add "est" to the end
- ✓ Adjectives that end in "y" add the ending "iest"
- ✓ Adjectives with two or more syllables add "most or least" before the adjective
- ✓ Some adjectives are irregular

Adjective	Question	Statement
	WH-Q + verb + <u>the + superlative</u> + (object).	(subject) + verb + <u>the + superlative</u> + (object).
(Fast ➜ Fast<u>est</u>)	What is <u>the fastest</u> sports car?	My car is <u>the fastest</u> sports car.
(Scary ➜ Scar<u>iest</u>)	What is <u>the scariest</u> movie?	The Ring is <u>the scariest</u> horror movie.
(Intelligent ➜ <u>Most intelligent</u>)	Who is <u>the most intelligent</u> scientist?	Einstein was <u>the most intelligent</u> scientist.
(Intelligent ➜ <u>least intelligent</u>)	Who is <u>the least intelligent</u> scientist?	Harper was <u>the least intelligent</u> scientist.
(Good ➜ <u>Best</u>)	When is <u>the best</u> time to eat ice-cream?	Ice-cream tastes <u>the best</u> when it is cold.

Practice: Look at the photos of animals again. In pairs, ask and answer superlative questions using these ideas.

Adjective	Object	Question:	Answer:
1. Hairy	Mammal	Which mammal is the hairiest?	The wolf is the hairiest mammal?
2. Scary	Animal	_____________________	_____________________
3. Dangerous	Hunter	_____________________	_____________________
4. Poisonous	Animal	_____________________	_____________________
5. Smallest	Creature	_____________________	_____________________
6. Delicious	To eat	_____________________	_____________________
7. Good	Pet	_____________________	_____________________
8. Bad	Gift	_____________________	_____________________

2. Comparative
- ✓ Adjectives with one syllable add "er" to the end
- ✓ Adjectives that end in "y" add the ending "ier"
- ✓ Adjectives with two or more syllables add "more" or "less" before the adjective
- ✓ Some adjectives are irregular

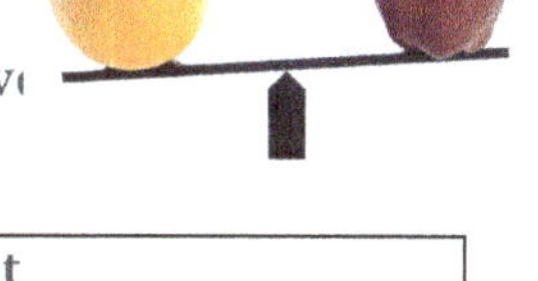

Adjective	Question	Statement
	WH-Q (object)+ verb + the + <u>comparative</u> Be-verb + (subject) <u>comparative + than</u> (object)?	(subject) + verb + <u>comparative + than</u> + (object).
(Fast ➜ Fast<u>er</u>)	Which sports car is <u>faster</u>? Is your car <u>faster than</u> mine?	My car is <u>faster than</u> your car.

(Scary ➔ Scar<u>ier</u>)	What movie is <u>scarier</u> movie? Is The Ring <u>scarier than</u> The Conjuring?	The Ring is <u>scarier than</u> The Conjuring.
(Intelligent ➔ <u>More</u> intelligent)	Which scientist is <u>more intelligent</u>? Is Einstein <u>more intelligent than</u> Edison?	Einstein was <u>more intelligent than</u> Edison.
(Intelligent ➔ <u>Less</u> intelligent)	Which scientist is <u>less intelligent</u>? Is Einstein <u>less intelligent than</u> Edison?	Edison was <u>less intelligent than</u> Einstein.
(Good ➔ <u>Better</u>)	What time is better to eat ice-cream? Is cold ice-cream <u>better than</u> warm ice-cream?	Cold Ice-cream tastes <u>better than</u> warm ice-cream

Practice: In pairs, ask and answer comparative questions using these ideas.

Subject	**Adjective**	**Object**	
1. Strawberry	Sweet	Orange	**Question:** Which fruit is <u>sweeter</u>? **Question:** Are strawberries sweeter than oranges? **Answer:** Strawberries are <u>sweeter than</u> oranges
2. Pasta	Delicious	Pizza	Q: _________________________________ A: _________________________________
3. Chrome	Useful	Internet Explorer	Q: _________________________________ A: _________________________________
4. BMW	Luxurious	Lexus	Q: _________________________________ A: _________________________________
5. McDonalds	Unhealthy	Fried Chicken	Q: _________________________________ A: _________________________________
6. Baseball	Exciting	Soccer	Q: _________________________________ A: _________________________________

<u>Conversation Practice</u>

Discuss your opinions about the topics below. For each topic, try to make a superlative or comparative question. Then express your opinions freely using either grammar points.

Topics:

International Food

Samsung VS Apple smartphones

Family pets

World leaders

Movies or TV dramas

Places to travel

Lesson 14: Life Complaints

Warm up: Describe the best day of your life. What happened?

Vocabulary

Psychiatrist	Come in	messed up
Lost	cubicle	
Catch up	every single	

Listening Comprehension 

Watch first: As you watch the video, listen and try to get the main ideas.

- What does Bill want Peter to do?

- How does Peter feel about his life?

Listen for Details: Now listen again and fill in the blanks with vocabulary words as you listen.

 Bill: Hello Peter. What's happening? Umm, I'm gonna need you to go ahead and come in tomorrow. So if you could be here around 9, that would be great. Mmmkay? Oh, oh and I almost forgot. Umm, I'm also gonna need you to go ahead and come in on Sunday too. We _______ some people this week, and we need to sort of play _______. Thanks.

- Does your boss tell you to work overtime? How about at your previous job?

Peter: So I was sitting in my _________ and I realized, ever since I started working, every single day of my life has been worse than the day before it. So that means every single day that you see me, that's on the worst day of my life.

Psychiatrist: What about today? Is today the worse day of your life?

Peter: Yeah.

Psychiatrist: Wow that's ___________. Sorry.

- How often do you complain to your friends/family/coworkers?

- What was the worst day at your job? What happened?

Grammar Focus

Irregular Comparative & Superlatives:

- ✓ Comparative Structure: **(subject 1)** verb + <u>comparative</u> + **(subject 2)**

- ✓ Superlative Structure: **(subject)** verb + <u>superlative</u> + **noun**

Adjective	Comparative	Superlative	Question & Answer
good	better than	the best	**Q:** Who is the best **player**?
bad	worse than	the worst	**A:** Michael is the best **player**.
little	less than	the least	**Q:** Does **Bill** have less than **Steve**?
much	more than	the most	**A:** Yes, **Bill** has less skill than **Steve**.
far	further than	the furthest	**Q:** Which **city** is farther, **LA** or **New York**?
			A: **New York** is farther than **LA.**

Practice 1: Use the images to ask and answer questions using the superlative form.

Example:
Q: I want to go to South Africa. Which **transportation** is better?
A: The cruise ship is better. It's the most luxurious!

Comparative

Q: _______________________________________

A: _______________________________________

Superlative

Q: _______________________________________

A: _______________________________________

Example:
Q: You tried a lot of exotic food. Which **animal** is worst?
A: French snail is worst. It is worse than **frog legs**.

Comparative

Q: _______________________________________

A: _______________________________________

Superlative

Q: _______________________________________

A: _______________________________________

Example:
Q: Which **landmark** have you seen <u>the most</u>?
A: I've visited China many times.
      So I've seen **the great wall** <u>the most.</u>

Comparative

Q: _________________________________

A: _________________________________

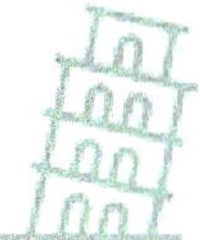  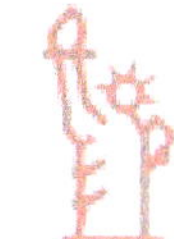

Superlative

Q: _________________________________

A: _________________________________

<u>Dialogue: Complaining Contest</u>

Read the list of relationships and scenarios. In pairs, choose your role and complain to your partner about your situation. Be ready to share your partner's complaints with the class.

Work

<u>Student A:</u> Your coworker makes many mistakes in a very important project.

<u>Student B:</u> Your boss is very authoritative and tells you to do things you don't want to do.

Hotel

<u>Student A:</u> You had a horrible experience at a hotel last night. You are going to complain to the staff.

<u>Student B:</u> You work at very popular hotel. You are working at the front desk when someone comes to complain.

Neighbor

<u>Student A:</u> A new neighbor just moved in above and they are making a lot of noise.

<u>Student B:</u> Your neighbor owns A LOT of pets, which are out of control.

Lesson 15: Outdated Technology

Warm up: What is your favorite piece of technology?

What do you use it for and how often do you use it?

Vocabulary

system	replace	outdated
developed	research	history
dominate	considerable	transfer
market	drop	superior
release	reported	format
almost	focus	boasting
completely		quality

Listening Comprehension  https://www.oneworldkorea.com/mc---beginner---session-2.html

Watch first: As you watch the video, listen and try to get the main ideas.

1. What time period was VHS dominant?

2. What replaced VHS and when?

3. Who uses VHS the most and what was the most recent VHS movie released?

4. Why is DVD superior to VHS?

Listen for Details: Now listen again and fill in the blanks with vocabulary words as you listen.

The video home system or VHS was developed by Victor Company of Japan in the _________________.
The VHS would _________________ the home video market in the 80s and 90s _________________ the
release of the DVD in 1997. Almost completely replacing the VHS by 2008. _________________.

-   Did you ever use VHS? When did you start using DVD?

As of 2013, according to research, close to 50% of Americans _________________ use VHS players
and tapes. It is a considerable _________________ from the reported 80% of Americans in 2005. We
focus a little on the American users for this _________________ piece of technological history
simply because they are _________________ the largest users and produced their last VHS release in
2007: The move Aragon. Most other countries almost completely transferred their media use to the
_________________ DVD format, boasting a better sound and video quality.

-   Do people in your country still use VHS or DVD?

Grammar Focus
1. Still & Until

Rule	Question	Sentence
"still" is an adverb that refers to a continuing situation	<u>Do</u> you **still** <u>meet</u> your friends from high school?	I **still** <u>meet</u> my friends from high school every weekend.
Negatives with **"still"** suggests that the situation should have changed but it has not	<u>Have</u> you **still not** <u>found</u> your passport?	I have been searching for hours, but I **still** <u>haven't found</u> my passport.
"until" is a preposition used to mark when something ends	**Until when** <u>does</u> the movie <u>show</u>?	The movie <u>doesn't end</u> **until** midnight.
"until" can be a conjunction used to connect an action to a point in time	**Until when** <u>did</u> he <u>work</u> in a factory?	He worked in a factory **until** <u>he retired in 1995</u>.

Practice: Think of items to add to the list below. Then in pairs discuss the questions.

Things you liked during high school:
- Fashion: _______________
- Music _______________
- Food _______________
- Movies _______________

- Technology _______________
- Books _______________
- People _______________
- Colors _______________

1: Do you still use _____________ now?

2. Until when did you use _______________?

2. "Used to" for Past Tense Habits

Rule	*Question*	*Sentence*
We use "used to" to tell stories about repeated actions or events in the past.	What did you <u>used to do</u> for fun in Europe? What <u>used to happen</u> if you got a bad score? What rule <u>used to exist</u> during the Chosun Dynasty?	When I lived in Europe, I <u>used to go</u> on a bike ride every Saturday. When I was young, teachers <u>used to hit</u> students if we got a bad score. During the Chosun Dynasty some men <u>used to have</u> more than one wife.
Add "not" after "used to" for negative statements.	What did your parents <u>used to not allow</u>? What did you <u>used to not like</u> eating? What did Steve <u>used to not study</u>?	My parents <u>used to not allow me</u> to eat candy when I was growing up. I <u>used to not like</u> eating mushrooms, but now I love them. Steve <u>used to not study</u> hard in English class but now he regrets it.

Practice: In pairs, finish the following sentences using the given topics.

1. **Time:** During the 1920s...   **Topic:** Music player
                                              Example: People <u>used to listen</u> to record players.
                                              Example: Musicians <u>used to not</u> have electric guitars.

2. **Time:** During the 1990s...   **Topic:** Telephones

____

____

3. **Time:** When you were
           in middle school...   **Topic:** Data storage

____

____

4. **Time:** When you were born...   **Topic:** Cameras

____

____

5. **Time:** When you were
           in university...   **Topic:** Popular musicians

____

____

6. **Time:** During the 1970s   **Topic:** Fashion & Hair styles

____

____

<u>Story Telling</u>

Share stories about the following topics, try to use past tense verbs, and "used to +(verb)" in your story. Takes notes on your partners story and be ready to explain their story to the whole class.

> ➤ What did you <u>used to do</u> before GPS/Navigation?

> ➤ When you were young, what video games did you <u>used to play</u>?

> ➤ How differently did people <u>used to live</u> before smart phones?

> ➤ When you were a student (elementary, high school or university), how did you <u>used to find</u> information?

Lesson 16: Haunted Hotel

Warm-Up: Where do you like to stay when you go on vacation?

- ☐ Pension   ☐ Guesthouse   ☐ Friend/Family house
- ☐ Hotel   ☐ Hostel   ☐ Camping

Vocabulary:

Haunted	Tune	Clanking
Accident	Get to bed	Whistle
Notoriously	Ghost	Scary
	Celebrity	

Listening Comprehension

https://www.oneworldkorea.com/mc---beginner---session-2.html

Watch first: As you watch the video, listen and try to get the main ideas.
- Why was Ellie staying at the hotel?
- What two things happened when Ellie was in bed?
- Was Ellie scared?

Now listen again and fill in the blanks with vocabulary words as you listen.

Ellen: You're in Seattle and you check into a hotel that's known for being ___________________. Everyone says it's haunted

Ellie: Everyone says it's haunted but I was there for work, so this is the hotel where they put us up, so I didn't have a choice. And it was a haunted hotel. _______________________ haunted.

Ellen: What's the name of it?

Ellie: It's the Sorrento Hotel. Now I hope they don't get mad. They know it's haunted. They're proud of it.

- Would you stay in a hotel if you knew it was haunted?
- Are there any places that are notoriously haunted in your country?

Ellie: And there had been some, you know, people had been seeing things, hearing things, other actors staying in the hotel. And one night I was going to bed and I was on the 8th floor. And there was a ballroom, conference room above me. And I was hearing all of this _____________________ around. They were having a party upstairs. So, there were lots of footsteps and tables moving and music and all this stuff.   So finally, about midnight, I said, I need to ___________________ to bed. I have an early call time. So I call the front desk and I said, excuse me, how long is this party going to go on? Well, you know the answer. .

Ellen: There was no party. . . .

Ellie: That's _________________.

Ellen: So then?

Ellie: And then I *did* go to bed. And I woke up 2 hours later and someone was whistling next to me.

Ellen: Like in bed next to you?

Ellie: Like in bed next to me, but there wasn't a person.

Ellen: What kind of _______________?

Ellie: It wasn't scary, like haunting. It was like a _______________ you would whistle to on the way to work, just (whistles). It was a sweet tune.

Ellen: But they don't have lips! How are they whistling?!

- Would you be scared in Ellie's situation?
- Do you believe that this was really a ghost or is there another explanation?

Grammar Focus
The Past Continuous + When & While

Use	Continuous Action	Specific Time
Actions that continued at a specific time in the past.	I <u>was watching</u> tv I <u>was failing</u> science class We <u>were talking</u> about our plans	*at 6pm* *in high school* *all day yesterday*

Use	Continuous Action 1	Action 2 interrupts Action 1
Actions that were interrupted by another action in the past	I was watching TV He was sleeping I was talking on the phone	**when** you **came** home. **when** there **was** a loud noise. **when** she **hit** me.

Use	Continuous Action 1	Parallel Action (while + Ving)
Two actions continuing at the same time in the past.	I <u>was watching</u> tv The movie <u>was playing</u> They <u>weren't listening</u>	**while** (I was) eat**ing** dinner. **while** he was sleep**ing**. **while** I was talk**ing**.

Practice 1: Make practice sentences with the images below. Try to use all three types

<u>**Practice Activity: Interrogation**</u>

Thieves robbed a house last night and the police are asking questions to neighbors hoping to find clues. In pairs play the roles of police detectives and witnesses. Start with the example structures and then add more of your own questions. Be creative!

<u>Actions at a specific time</u>

What noise did you hear at **10:00pm**.

Where were you at ____________________________ (time)?

Who were you with at ____________________________ (time)?

<u>Interrupted actions</u>

Where were you when **the alarm started to ring**?

What were you doing when ____________________________?

Why were you _________ when ____________________________?

<u>Parallel actions</u>

While you were **getting in your car**, who were you **talking to**?

While you were ______________ what were you ____________________________?

While ______________ was happening, where was/were ____________________________?

<u>Conversation</u>: Storytelling about your experiences

- ✓ Choose an experience you have
- ✓ Explain it to your partner using the past continuous
- ✓ Ask questions to get *specific* details
- ✓ Be ready to share you partner's story with the class

Saw/heard a Ghost	**Cried during a movie**
Had / Saw a car accident	**Talked on the phone for more than 2 hours**
Met / Seen a celebrity	**Helped someone in danger**
Got caught in bad weather	**Made someone cry**
Found money	**Drove for more than 6 hours**
Overslept	**Lost something**

Lesson 17: Magic Matchmaker

Warm up: Have you ever seen a dating or match making TV show? Do you think some ways of meeting a partner can be more successful than others? Consider:

☐ Meeting at Work   ☐ Childhood Friends   ☐ Meeting in a Bar

☐ Blind Date   ☐ Meeting at School   ☐ Online Dating

Vocabulary

mirror	bachelorette	livewire
kingdom	abused	fiery
technically	fancy	lava
eligible	frozen	rescue

Listening Comprehension

https://www.oneworldkorea.com/mc---beginner---session-2.html

Watch the video and listen for details to fill in the blanks with vocabulary words.

Knight: My lord, we found it.

Farquad: Well then what are you waiting for? Bring it in. Magic mirror... [Good] Evening. Mirror, mirror on the wall is this not the most perfect _______________________ of them all?

Mirror: Well, technically you're not a king...   **Farquad:** Uh Thelonious? You were saying...

Mirror: What I mean is that you're not a king yet but, but you can become one. All you have to do is marry a _______________________.   **Farquad:** Go on.

Mirror: Huh, so just sit back and relax my lord because it's time for you to meet today's eligible bachelorettes and here they are: Bachelorette number one is a mentally abused shut-in from a kingdom far, far away. She likes sushi and hot tubbing anytime. Her hobbies include cooking and cleaning for two evil sisters. Please welcome _______________! Bachelorette number two is a cape-wearing girl from the land of fancy. Although she lives with seven other men, she's not easy. Just kiss her dead, frozen lips and find out what a livewire she is. Come on and give it up for ___________ _______________! And last but certainly not least, bachelorette number three is a fiery redhead from a dragon-guarded Castle surrounded by hot boiling lava. But don't let that cool you off. She's a loaded pistol who likes pina coladas and getting caught in the rain. Yours for the rescuing, Princess _______________! So who will it be? Bachelorette number one, bachelorette number two, or bachelorette number three?

Knights: One! Two! Three! Pick number three, my lord!   **Farquad:** Okay, okay. Number three.

Mirror: Lord Farquad *you've chosen* Princess Fiona.   **Farquad:** Princess Fiona, she's perfect....

- Which Bachelorette do you think is the best choice and why?

- Do you think that matchmaking is a good way for a person to find a spouse?

Grammar Focus

Present perfect tense for experiences

✓ Means an unspecified time before now.

✓ Use Has/Have Past Participle for the verb

✓ Negative form adds "never" or "n't" after Has/Have

✓ Contractions can be used like "I've", "He's", "They've"

Question	Positive Sentence	Negative Sentence
Has/Have + Subject + **P.P.** + Object	Subject + **Has/Have P. P.** + Object	Subject + **Has/Have never P. P.** + Object Subject + **Hasn't/Haven't P. P.** + Object
Have they **been** to Paris?	They **have been** to Paris.	They **have never been** to Paris. They **haven't been** to Paris.
Have you **eaten** dog meat?	I **have eaten** dog meat.	I **have never eaten** dog meat. I **haven't eaten** dog meat.
Has he **stolen** something?	He **has stolen** my pencil.	He **has never stolen** anything. He **hasn't stolen** anything.

Practice & Discussion: Use the verbs and objects to make past perfect questions. Then ask follow up questions to your partner. Take notes on what your partner says. You will share 2 interesting facts about your partner to the whole class.

Example:

go + skydiving ➔ A: **Have** you **gone** skydiving?   B: No I **haven't gone** skydiving.

A: Why haven't you gone skydiving?   B: Because I am too scared!

1. be + to a foreign country   Q1: _______________________________________

Q2: _______________________________________

2. eat + Brazilian food   Q1: _______________________________________

Q2: _______________________________________

3. speak + to a fortune teller Q1: _______________________________________

Q2: _______________________________________

4. drink + scotch whiskey   Q1: _______________________________________

Q2: _______________________________________

5. wear + fake hair

Q1: _______________________________________

Q2: _______________________________________

6. steal + something

Q1: _______________________________________

Q2: _______________________________________

7. Ride + bicycle

Q1: _______________________________________

Q2: _______________________________________

8. get + in trouble

Q1: _______________________________________

Q2: _______________________________________

9. break + bone

Q1: _______________________________________

Q2: _______________________________________

10. drive + motorcycle

Q1: _______________________________________

Q2: _______________________________________

Most Commonly used Irregular Past Participle Verbs

Base-Verb	Simple Past	P.P	Base-Verb	Simple Past	P.P	Base-Verb	Simple Past	P.P
begin	began	begun	fall	fell	fallen	ride	rode	ridden
break	broke	broken	fly	flew	flown	see	saw	seen
choose	chose	chosen	forget	forgot	forgotten	sing	sang	sung
do	did	done	get	got	gotten	speak	spoke	spoken
draw	drew	drawn	give	gave	given	steal	stole	stolen
drink	drank	drunk	go	went	gone	take	took	taken
drive	drove	driven	grow	grew	grown	wear	wore	worn
eat	ate	eaten	know	knew	known	write	wrote	written

Lesson 18: Restaurant Complaint

Warm up: When you go out to eat, how important is good service to you?

Vocabulary

specials	kill	kitchen
complained	embarrassed	law
taste buds	meal	atmosphere
fresh	spit	

Listening Comprehension 

https://www.oneworldkorea.com/mc---beginner---session-2.html

Watch first: As you watch the video, listen and try to get the main ideas.

3. Where did she go and who did she go with?

4. What was the problem?

5. Why was Natalie so embarrassed?

Listen for Details: Now listen again and fill in the blanks with vocabulary words as you listen.

Friend: Ugh. This is awful.
Nataile: Is it?
Friend: What's yours. How is it?
Natalie: Umm, it's like chicken. It's alright.
Friend: Nah, that's ________________. That's not chicken.
Natalie: Is it? God, I have no ________. I once ate a button...
Friend: Excuse me, waiter?
Natalie: What are you doing?
Friend: I'm gonna ____________.
Natalie: No, don't ____________!
Friend: Excuse me, waiter. Yeah, hi. Sorry, I'm just not very happy with my meal.
Natalie: Oh, ____________ me now.
Friend: Um, I feel like it doesn't taste very ____________ or something.
Natalie: My friend's not happy with hers either.
Waiter: I'm very sorry to hear that, I'll have another two ____________ made up for you.
Natalie: Now they are going to ____________ in our food.
Friend: What?
Natalie: Now that you told them you don't like the food, what do you think is going to happen?
They are going to go back in the ____________ and they're going to spit in the new food.
Friend: Says who?
Natalie: Says everybody. It's the ____________.

-   Do you ever complain if you receive bad service or food at a restaurant?

-   Do you agree with Natalie that complaining makes the chef angry?

-   What is the worst restaurant you've gone to? Why was it so bad (food, service, atmosphere)?

Grammar Focus
Too & Enough
- ✓ 'Enough' comes after an Adjective or before a noun to say that quality or quantity is *okay*
- ✓ 'Not + Adjective/Noun + Enough' say that something is *less* than what is needed
- ✓ 'Too' to say that something is *more* than needed

enough + <u>noun</u>	**adjective + enough**
I have **enough** <u>time</u> to help you this evening.	Bob is **tall enough** to reach the basket.
not enough + <u>noun</u>	**not + <u>adjective</u> + enough**
The man wants to buy the car but he does**n't** have **enough** <u>money</u>.	The blanket is**n't** <u>big</u> **enough**. My coffee is**n't** <u>hot</u> **enough**. Please heat it again.
too much/many + <u>noun</u>	**too + <u>adjective</u>**
The boy ate 10 scoops of ice cream and then vomited. He ate **too much** <u>ice cream</u>.	The classroom is **too** <u>hot</u>. Please open the window. His pillow is **too** <u>hard</u>. He can't sleep.

1. Practice: Look at the photos and try to make at least two sentences for each using the grammar.

    Examples:

The cat has **too much** <u>weight</u>.
He does**n't** get **enough** <u>exercise</u>.
He looks **too** <u>fat</u>.
He is**n't** <u>healthy</u> **enough**.

2. Practice: Brainstorm with the teacher. Think of common places to complain. Then, in pairs, choose one and brainstorm adjectives that you can use in a dialogue. Then role play your complaint.

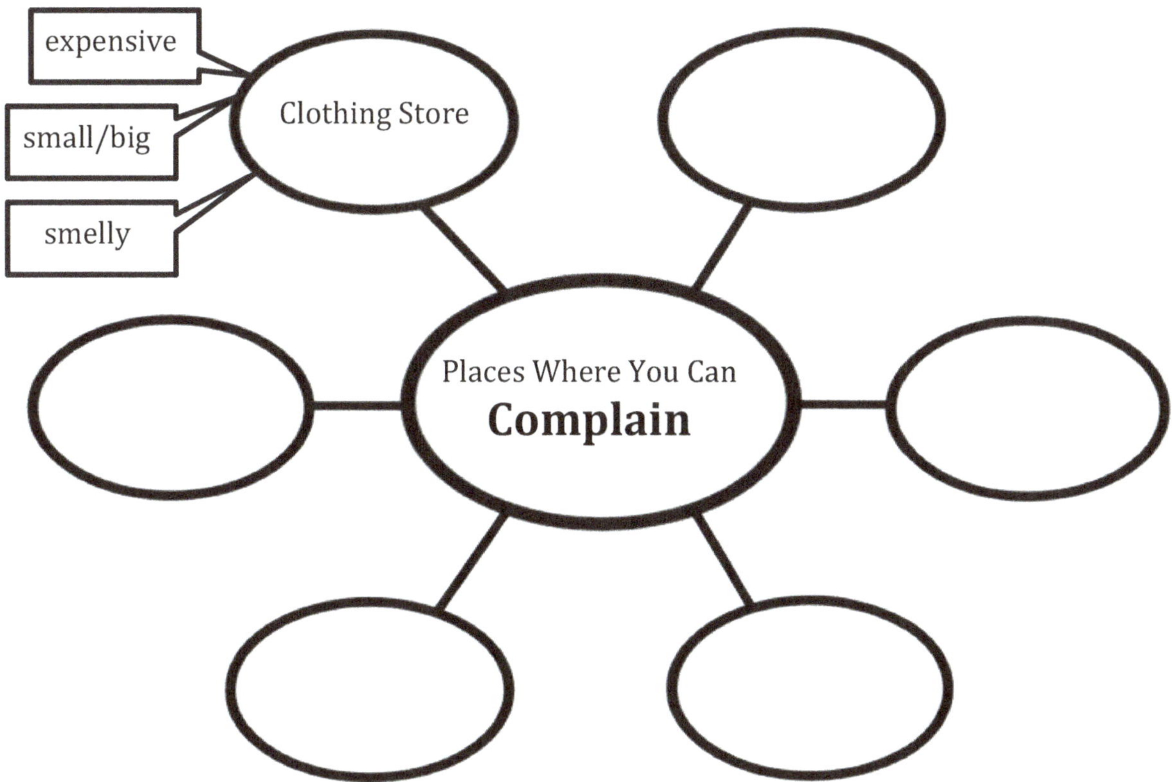

<u>**Example:**</u>
Place: Cafe
Adjectives: hot, cold, expensive, sweet, bitter, late, fast, awful, horrible

Customer: Excuse me. I'm sorry but my latte is **too <u>cold</u>**.
Server: I'm so sorry to hear that. I will make you a new one. Is there anything else?
Customer: Yes, actually. The TV is **not <u>loud</u> enough**. Could you turn it up?
Server: Okay. No problem.

> **Useful phrases**
> **Customer:**
>   Excuse me but..
>   Sorry but...
> **Business Owner**
>   I'm so sorry ma'am/sir.
>   I'm sorry to hear that.

Activity: What am I complaining about?

Using one of the places from the brainstorm, think of something to complain about. Use too+adj/not+adj+enough to complain about your without saying exactly what it is. The other students must correctly guess what item you are complaining about.

<u>**Example:**</u>
Place: Hi-Mart
Object: Oven

Customer: Hi, I would like to return this product.
Clerk: Well, what is the problem?
Customer: I want to bake pizza, but it is **not <u>wide</u> enough.**
Clerk: Okay, any other problems
Customer: Yes, it has **too many <u>buttons</u>**.
Clerk....
Customer...

Lesson 19: Restaurant Service

Warm up: How often do you eat at fast food hamburger restaurants?

What do you usually order?

Do you usually get your meal "Biggy-size"?

Vocabulary

"hold an ingredient"	"give someone lip"	break
spit	handle	fool
quarter	beverage	relax
punch	liter	

Listening Comprehension

Watch first: As you watch the video**, listen and try to get the main ideas.**

- What joke does the clerk tell Officer Farva?

- What does the clerk want to sell to Officer Farva?

- Why does Officer Farva attack the clerk?

Listen for Details: Now listen again and fill in the blanks with vocabulary words as you listen.

Officer Farva: Give me a, uh, pie. Apple.

Clerk: Do you want me to hold the ___________________? Ha ha. Just kidding Officer Farva.
So, um, do you want to "Dippy-size" your meal for a __________________ more?

Officer Farva: Want me to punchy-size your face for free?

Officer Ramathorn: Some male figure? I'm his dad, and stop with the whole transfer thing.
You know what? I've gotta go. Let's talk about this later. Okay, bye.

Officer Farva: Now don't give me any _______________.

Clerk: It's just a quarter and look how much more you get.

Officer Farva: I said NO!

Clerk: It's just ______________ __________________.

Officer Ramathorn: Listen guy, he doesn't want it.

Officer Farva: I can ________________ this Ramathorn. I don't want it!

- Have you ever met a rude clerk?

- Do people in your country have great respect for police officers?

Clerk: Alright. A _________________?

Officer Farva: Give me a, uh, liter of cola.

Clerk: A what?

Officer Farva: A _________________ of cola.

Clerk: "Literocola"? Do we make "literocola"?

Officer Ramathorn: Just order a large, Farva.

Officer Farva: I don't want a large Farva. I want a Goddamn liter of cola.

Clerk: I don't know what that is.

Officer Farva: Liter is French for give me some f*ing cola before I break fool's f*ing lips!

Clerk: Alright, alright. Relax.

Officer Farva: Does that look like _____________ to you.

Officer Ramathorn: Yeah.

- How would you react in this situation?

Grammar Focus

1. **Want, Want to, Want someone to**

   ✓ Use the verb "want" to talk about wishes and needs.

   ✓ Can be used directly with nouns

   ✓ Add "to" when using it with verbs

   ✓ "Want someone to" is used to tell people to do something

   ✓ Use "don't want" for negative sentences

   ✓ Add "do" to questions

Want + (object)	Want to + (verb)	Want someone to + (verb)
I want a beer.	I want to drink wine.	I want you to drink wine.
She wants money.	She wants to have money.	She wants her husband to earn money.
They don't want trouble.	They don't want to watch TV.	They don't want Frank to leave.
Do you want cake?	When do you want to eat?	What do you want me to do?

Practice Part 1: In pairs ask and answer the following questions and discuss why.

1. What product do you want?

2. When do you want to retire from work?

3. Where do you not want to travel?

4. Do you want your company to send you to a foreign country to work?

2. **Service and Ordering Language**

<u>Practice Role Play</u>: In pairs, use the example below to order food from the menu:

Clerk: Hello, how may I help you?	**Clerk:** Hello, how may I help you?
Customer: I would like a Pizza.	**Customer:** I would like a ______________.
Clerk: Sorry but we don't have pizza, we are a Chinese restaurant we only have Chinese food.	**Clerk:** Sorry but we don't have______________, we ______________.
Customer: Alright, then please give me *sweet and sour pork*.	**Customer:** Alright, then please give me __________________.
Clerk: Okay, would you like a side dish?	**Clerk:** Okay, would you like__________________?
Customer: Yes, please give me two *spring rolls*.	**Customer:** Yes, please give me__________________
Clerk: Do you want to drink soda?	**Clerk:** Do you want to drink ________________?
Customer: No, I don't want cola. I just want *water*.	**Customer:** ________________________________.
Clerk: Okay, so you want one *sweet and sour pork, two spring rolls, and one water. Is that correct?*	**Clerk:** Okay, so you want ________________________ ________________________________. *Is that correct?*
Customer: *Yes, thanks.*	**Customer:** *Yes, thanks.*
Clerk: *That will be $60.*	**Clerk:** *That will be* ______________.
Customer: *What!? Are you kidding?*	**Customer:** ________________!

FAMOUS BURGERS   FAMOUS FRIES

HAMBURGER
CHEESEBURGER
BACON BURGER
BACON CHEESEBURGER
LITTLE HAMBURGER
LITTLE CHEESEBURGER
LITTLE BACON BURGER
LITTLE BACON CHEESEBURGER

100% KOSHER HOT DOG
CHEESE or BACON DOG
BACON CHEESE DOG
VEGGIE or GRILLED CHEESE

REGULAR
LARGE

Cooked in pure, no cholesterol, tasty peanut oil !

DRINKS
24 oz.
free refills

Coca Cola products

ALL TOPPINGS FREE:

**Mayo   Relish*   Onions*   Lettuce   Pickles   Tomatoes   Fried Onions
Sauteed Mushrooms   Ketchup   Mustard   Jalapeno Peppers*
Green Peppers   A-1 Sauce*   Bar-B-Q Sauce*   Hot Sauce***
**Upon request only*

Lesson 20: Not Gonna Go

Warm up: Why did you choose to work in your career field?

Vocabulary:

cubicle	bills	take (sb) out
switch	get fired	quit
digits	anymore	come over
lines of code	(sth) matters	decide

Listening Comprehension 

Watch first: As you watch the video**, listen and try to get the main ideas.**

- Does Peter like his job?

- What does Peter want to do?

Listen for Details: Now listen again and fill in the blanks with vocabulary words as you listen.

Joanna: So, where do you, uh, work Peter?
Peter: Initech.
Joanna: Ini--, ah what do you do there?
Peter: I sit in a _______________________ and I update bank software for the 2000 switch.
Joanna: What's that?
Peter: Well you see, they wrote all this bank software and to save space, they use two _____________________ for the date instead of four, so, like '98 instead of 1998. So I go through these thousands of lines of ____________________ and uh, it doesn't really ____________________. I, uh, I don't like my job. And I don't think I'm gonna go anymore.

- What is Peter's job? Would you like doing this job?

Joanna: You're just not gonna go?
Peter: Yeah.
Joanna: Won't you get _________________?
Peter: I don't know. But I really don't like it and I'm not gonna go.
Joanna: So, you're gonna _______________?
Peter: No, not really. I'm just gonna stop going.
Joanna: When did you _________________ all of that?
Peter: About an hour ago.
Joanna: Really? So you're gonna get another job?
Peter: I don't think I'd like another job.
Joanna: What are you gonna do about money and ___ and . . .
Peter: You know, I never really liked paying bills. I don't think I'm gonna do that either.

- Mark which statements are true (T) or false (F). If the sentence is false, explain why.

T / F - Peter is going to quit his job.   T / F - Peter is going to pay all of his bills.

T / F - Peter is going to get fired.   T / F - Peter is going to go to work tomorrow.

T / F - Peter is going to get another job.

Grammar Focus:

Future Plans & Predictions

- ✓ **Going to + infinitive** can be used to describe future plans or future predictions
- ✓ **"going to"** is often shortened to **"gonna"** in spoken conversation

Future Plans

Subject	be	going to + base verb	not going to + base verb
I	**am**	going to <u>wake</u> up early tomorrow going to <u>work</u> tomorrow	not going to <u>wake</u> up early tomorrow not going to <u>work</u> tomorrow
He / She	**is**	going to <u>go</u> on vacation going to <u>get</u> a new job	not going to <u>go</u> on vacation not going to <u>get</u> a new job
We / You / They	**are**	going to <u>see</u> a movie going to <u>get</u> married	not going to <u>see</u> a movie not going to <u>get</u> married

Future predictions

Subject	be	going to + base verb	not going to + base verb
I	**am**	going to <u>miss</u> the train going to <u>be</u> lucky	not going to <u>miss</u> the train not going to <u>lose</u>
He / She / It	**is**	going to <u>rain</u> tonight going to <u>be</u> angry	not going to <u>rain</u> tonight not going to <u>be</u> happy
We / You / They	**are**	going to <u>live</u> forever going to <u>be</u> rich	not going to <u>live</u> forever not going to <u>be</u> rich

Practice 1: In Pairs, look at the pictures below and make future sentences using "**going to + base verb**". Afterwards, mark which is a plan (**PL**) and which is a prediction (**PR**).

He is going to die from cold!

PR

____
____

Practice 2: In pairs, and make predictions about Peter's future (from the video-dialogue).

- When is Peter's boss going to fire him?
- Do you think Peter is going to be rich?
- Are Peter and Joanna going to get married?
- Is Peter going to be able to get another job?

Conversation: Life events

In pairs, ask questions and answer questions about the future topics below.   Consider these questions:

- ✓ **Which are you going to do? Which are you not going to do?**
- ✓ **When are you going to ______________? (Before you're 50, after you're 40, next year…)**
- ✓ **Why are you going to ___________? Why are you not going to ___________?**

Travel	Get a new job	Get married	Have children	Retire
Win the lottery	Buy a new house	Move to a new apartment	Get a new car	Learn a new hobby
Go on vacation	Go back to school	Get a promotion	Celebrate an anniversary	Have a class reunion

Lesson 21: Future Technology

Warm up: What do you plan to do 1 year/2 years/5 years from now?

Vocabulary

futurologists	factories	behavior
predict	medical technology	intelligence
fields of _____	blind	picture
directly	deaf	definite
replace	clone	

Listening Comprehension

https://www.oneworldkorea.com/mc---beginner---session-3.html

Watch First: As you watch the video, listen and try to get the main ideas.

- What kinds of advanced technology did you see?

- Which will media send directly to our TV sets?

- Where might we be able to see robots in 2050?

Listen for Details: Now listen again and fill in the blanks with vocabulary words as you listen.

What will life be like in 2050? What _________ do you have of the future? Will life be better, worse, or the same as now? ___________ predict that life will probably be very different in 2050 in all ________ activity. [Digital Room Key] [Your Room is Ready].

- Do you think life will be better, worse, or the same as now? Why?

Robots will be everywhere. Schools, offices, hospitals, shops and homes, and they will ________ people in factories. _____________ will help _______ people to see, and ______ people to hear. Scientists will be able to ________ people and decide on their appearance, _________ and _________. But, should they?

- Will robots replace people? Will technology heal disabled people? Will humans be able to clone? Why or why not?

- Should humans clone people and decide on their appearance?

Grammar Focus

Future tense "will"

- ✓ Used to talk about a *definite* future plan

- ✓ *Will* can be shortened to *'ll*

- ✓ *Will not* can be shortened to *won't*

Positive Sentences	Negative Sentences	Questions
Subject + Will + Base Verb	Subject + will not + Base Verb	[WH] + will + Subject + Base Verb?
He **will** meet his friends.	He **will not** talk to her anymore.	**Will** you join us this evening?
They **will** wake up at 9:00am.	They **won't** be ready at 7:00am.	**When will** you see the movie?
I**'ll** work at home tomorrow.	I **won't** buy that coat.	**Where'll** you go for vacation?

Practice 1: In pairs ask each other future questions using the times below.

- ➢ after class today
- ➢ this weekend
- ➢ at 8:00pm this evening

- ➢ during the next holiday
- ➢ when you retire
- ➢ in 10 years

Practice 2: In pairs look at the photos and discuss your ideas about "What will happen next?" Ask each other follow up questions to predict more future details.

Discussion: Future Solutions

In groups brainstorm ideas about how people will solve problems in the future. Ask and answer follow up questions about these problems using "will".

Example: World hunger

In the future, people **won't** be hungry. Scientists **will** invent a pill that people **will** take everyday. The pill **will** have all the vitamins and nutrients that people need. With the extra time saved, people **will** work more!

Topics: **Ideas:**

Too much stress   ______________________________________

Global Warming   ______________________________________

Air Pollution   ______________________________________

Expensive housing   ______________________________________

Disease   ______________________________________

Old Age   ______________________________________

Unhealthy eating   ______________________________________

Lack of exercise   ______________________________________

Bad eyesight   ______________________________________

Future Invention

Work in groups to create your own future technology, which will solve one of the problems you discussed above. Try to answer all of the questions below. After you are finished, be ready to share your inventions with the class.

- **What is the name of this invention?**
- **Who will use this?**
- **Why will people need this?**
- **When will we need this?**
- **Where will people use this?**
- **What will it look like?**
- **How much will it cost?**
- **What will it do?**

Lesson 22: Protective Father

Warm up: Were your parents very protective of you when you were growing up?

What were some rules that they had, which you needed to follow?

Did you live independently or with your parents after graduating high school?

Vocabulary

Related	Of course	Daughter
Prefer	Problem	Chance
Address (verb)	Excuse me	Change ones mind

Listening Comprehension  https://www.oneworldkorea.com/mc---beginner---session-3.html

Watch First: As you watch the video, listen and try to get the main ideas.

How are Paul and Ross related to Liz?

Why does Paul think Ross has a problem?

What is Paul giving Ross time to do?

Listen for Details: Now listen again and fill in the blanks with vocabulary words as you listen.

Liz: This is _________ ________________, Paul Stevens. Dad, this is Ross Geller.
Ross: It's great to meet you Paul.
Paul: I usually prefer that _________ _____________ address me as Mr. Stevens.
Ross: Of course, of course, Mr. Stevens.
- Do you think it is okay to call your boyfriend/girlfriends parents by first names?

Paul: So, Ross, what's ____________ ________________?
Ross: Excuse me?
Paul: Why can't you get a girlfriend _____________ own _____________?
Ross: It's funny… um. It's not funny.
- Is it okay to date someone who is much younger or older than you? How much is okay?

Paul: I don't like you going out with __________ ________________, Ross.
Ross: Okay, I can see that. But I think if you give me one chance, I can change your mind.
Paul: Okay. You've got one chance to change _________ ____________. You've got one minute.
Liz: Daddy.
Paul: Fine, two minutes. Go!
- Are fathers very protective of their daughters like this in your culture?

- Did your parents ever dislike one of your boyfriends/girlfriends?

Grammar Focus

1. Forming Possessives

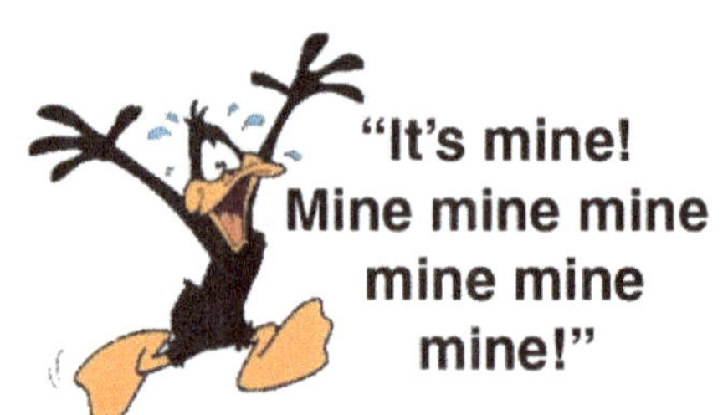

✓ Most singular nouns can become possessive by adding **'s**

✓ Singular nouns that already end in "s" can add only **'**

✓ Plural nouns that end in "s" can add only **'**

✓ Possessive Pronouns can be used in place of nouns

Noun + 's	Subject Pronouns	Sentence
The car's window	Its	**Its** window was broken.
Charles' book	His, her, my	**His** book is on the table.
The witches' brooms	Your, Our, Their	**Their** brooms are magical.
Noun + 's	Object Pronouns	Sentence
The car's window	Its	I broke **its window**
Charles' book	His, Hers, Mine	The book is **his.**
The witches' brooms	Yours, Ours, Theirs	The brooms are **theirs.**

<u>Practice 1</u>: Look at the photos and say what you like or don't like about their fashion.

Example: I don't like <u>**his**</u> eye patch.   Example: I want to buy a dress like <u>**hers.**</u>

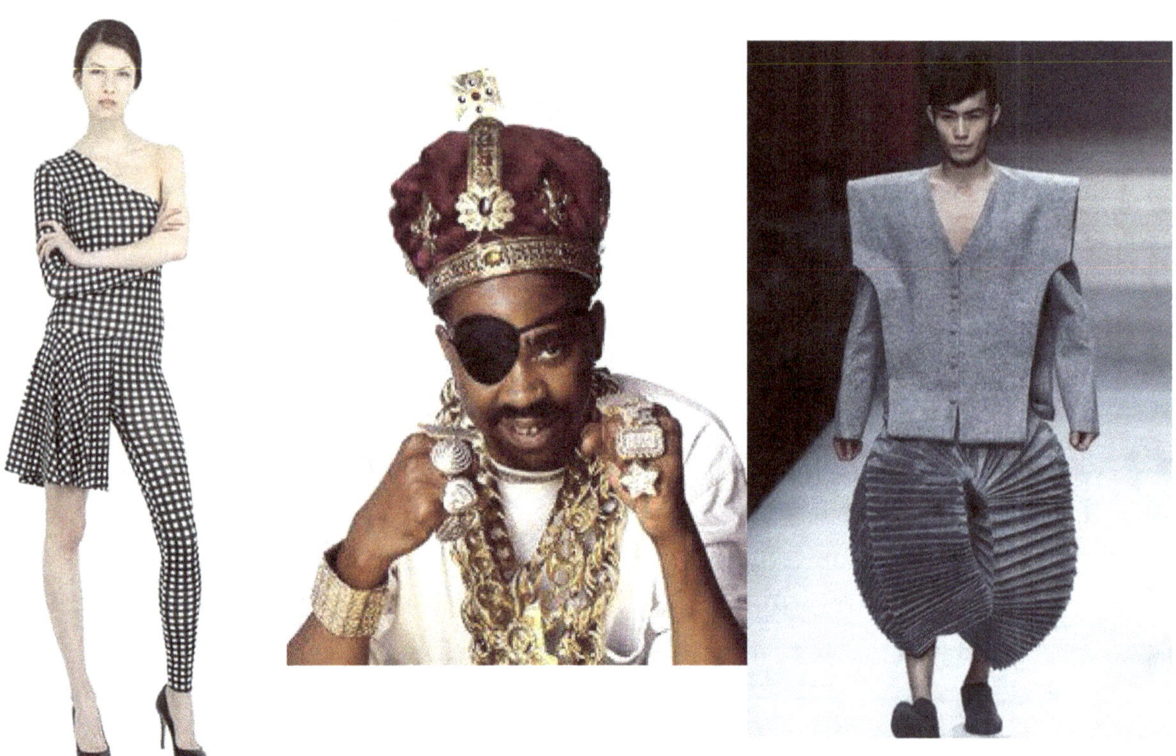

<u>Practice 2:</u> In pairs introduce one of your family members to your partner by answering this information about them:

What is his/her relationship to you?
What is his/her age?
What is his/her occupation?
What is his/her hobby?

Discussion

What should the ideal husband or wife have? Using the list below, select the 3 most important factors that you consider, when choosing someone to date or marry:

- ☐ His/her age
- ☐ His/her occupation
- ☐ His/her wealth
- ☐ His/her appearance
- ☐ His/her personality
- ☐ His/her family
- ☐ His/her friends
- ☐ His/her education
- ☐ His/her nationality
- ☐ His/her hobby

Now share your factors with your partner and discuss:

1. How are your choices similar or different?

2. Why did you choose factors in that way?

3. Which of these factors does your husband/wife/boyfriend/girlfriend/ex-partner have or not have?

Lesson 23: Fear vs Love

Warm Up: Whom do you have the closest relationship with? How did you meet your closest friends?

Vocabulary

Be feared	Availability	Treat (sb) good / bad
Be hated	Neighborhood	Trick
Make a joke	Last (a long/short time)	Otherwise
Friendship	Loyal	Think twice

Listening Comprehension  https://www.oneworldkorea.com/mc---beginner---session-3.html

Watch First: As you <u>watch the video</u>, listen and try to get the main ideas.

- What relationship is he talking about?

- Is choosing to be feared or loved an easy choice?

Listen for Details: Now listen again and fill in the blanks with vocabulary words as you listen.

Boss: That's what it comes down to, _______________. The people in this _______________ that see me every day, that are on my side, they feel safe because they know I'm close. That gives them more reason to love me. But the people that want to do _________________, they _________________ because they know I'm close. That gives them more reason to fear me.

Junior: Is it better to be loved or _____________?

Boss: That's a good question. It's nice to be both, but it's difficult. But if I had my choice, I <u>would rather be feared</u>. Fear ________________ longer than love. _________________ that are bought with money mean nothing. You see how it is around here. I make a ________________, everybody laughs. I know I'm funny, but I'm not that funny. It's fear that keeps them _______________ to me. But the trick is not to be ________________. That's why I _______________ my men good, but not too good. I give them too much, then they don't need me. I give them just enough where they need me, but they don't hate me. Don't forget what I'm telling you.

- Do you agree with this bosses idea of how to keep power?

- Which do you feel most about your boss, fear, love or hate?

- What are gangsters like in your country? Have you ever seen or interacted with them?

<u>**Grammar Focus:**</u>

Would Rather + Verb

- ✓ This phrase has the same meaning as "I like to (verb) more" and "I would prefer to (verb)"
- ✓ Can be abbreviated to **'d rather + verb**
- ✓ When comparing two choices, questions can use "or" or "than", and statements can use "than"

Questions	Answers
Would you **rather** <u>sleep</u> *than* <u>go</u> to the party?	Yes, I **would rather** sleep.
Why **would** you **rather** <u>drink</u> *than* <u>eat</u>?	Because drinking is more fun!
Where **would** you **rather** <u>go</u> *instead of* Guam?	**I'd rather** <u>go</u> to Hawaii.
What **would** she **rather** do, <u>surf</u> or <u>ski</u>?	I think she **would rather** <u>surf</u> *than* <u>ski</u>.
Who **would** you **rather** <u>fight</u>, Bob or Helen?	**I'd rather** <u>fight</u> Helen *than* Bob.
When **would** you **rather** <u>go</u>, morning or night?	**I'd rather** <u>go</u> at night.
How **would** you **rather** <u>pay</u>, cash or credit	I **would rather** <u>pay</u> in credit, please.

Practice 1: In pairs, use the images below to make questions and answers with "would rather". Ask follow up questions to explain your choices.

Q: ____

____

A: ____

____

Q: ____

____

A: ____

____

Q: _______________________________________

____

A: _______________________________________

____

Q: _______________________________________

____

A: _______________________________________

____

Q: _______________________________________

____

A: _______________________________________

____

<u>Conversation:</u>

- ➢ **Answer the following WOULD RATHER questions and explain why**

- ➢ **You can also say: Both / Either / Neither**

1. If you were a CEO, would you rather be feared than loved by your employees?

2. Would you rather have a lot of friends or a few friends?

3. Would you rather be stupid and happy or smart and unhappy?

4. Would you rather have more sleep or free time?

5. Would you rather travel domestically or travel in another country?

6. Would you rather read the book first or see the movie first?

7. Would you rather learn a new language or play a new instrument?

8. Would you rather win the lottery or win an Olympic gold medal?

Lesson 24: Fuzzy Memories

Warm up: What did you enjoy more, your life as a child, or your life now as an adult?

Vocabulary

fuzzy	pull out	run away
memory	butcher knife	yelling
favorite	sword	costume
pirate	pretend	
adult	suddenly	

Listening Comprehension

Watch First: As you watch the video, listen and try to get the main ideas.

- What was the speaker's favorite childhood game?

- How did they play this game?

- Until when did they continue to play this game?

Listen for Details: Now listen again and fill in the blanks with vocabulary words as you listen.

I remember when we were kids, one of our _______________ games was to play Pirate. We'd dress up like __________________. Then we'd find an adult walking down the street and we'd go up to him and pull out our butcher knives. Which we called "_________________" and say "We're pirates, give us your _________________." A lot of adults would ________________ to be scared and give us their money. Others would suddenly _____________ ______________ yelling for help. We played Pirate until we were _________________ or so.

- Did you like to play games with costumes when you were young or dress up for Halloween?

- Are the adults "pretending" to be scared or are they *actually* scared?

- Why do you think they continued to play until they were 20 years old?

- What would happen if kids really played this game?

Grammar Focus

1. Would for Past Tense Habits

Rule	*Examples*
We use would to tell stories about repeated actions or events in the past.	When I lived in Europe, I <u>would go</u> on a bike ride every Saturday. When I was young, teachers <u>would hit</u> students if we got a bad score. During the Chosun Dynasty some men would have more than one wife.
Add "not" after "would" for negative statements.	My parents <u>wouldn't allow me</u> to eat candy when I was growing up. My friend <u>would not talk</u> to me after I stole her boyfriend. Steve <u>wouldn't study</u> hard in English class but now he regrets it.
We can't use "would" in this way with states (live, exist). In these cases use "used to" instead.	NO: ~~We would live in America.~~ YES: We <u>used to live</u> in America. NO: ~~Dinosaurs would exist here.~~ YES: Dinosaurs <u>used to exist</u> here.
"Would" can't be used with other modals (must, can, might, should, could)	NO: My parents ~~would should pay~~ for my academy lessons. YES: My parents <u>would need to pay</u> for my academy lessons.

<u>Practice</u>: In pairs, finish the following sentences using the given topics.

1. In Europe during the 1800s...

Topic 1: Men's fashion

> **Example:** Men <u>would wear</u> wigs.
> Men would wear tight pants.

Topic 2: Women's fashion

> **Example:** Women <u>would wear</u> corsets.
> Women would wear long dresses.

2. In Asia during the 1800s...

Topic 1: Men's fashion

____

____

Topic 2: Women's fashion

____

____

3. When I was young...

Topic 1: Holiday Activity

____

____

Topic 2: After school routine

____

____

4. During the World Cup...

Topic 1: Special events/songs/clothes

____

____

Topic 2: Ways to celebrate

____

____

<u>Story Telling</u>

In pairs, choose a topic and share stories about it, try to use past tense verbs, "would+(verb)" and "used to" in your story. Takes notes on your partners story and be ready to explain their story to the whole class.

- ➢ When you were young, what <u>would happen</u> if you got a bad test score?

- ➢ When you were young, what games <u>would</u> you <u>play</u> often?

- ➢ When you were starting your first job, how <u>would</u> you <u>spend</u> your first paychecks.

- ➢ When you were a student (elementary, high school or university), what <u>would</u> you <u>care about</u> most? (grades, money, dating, fashion, friends, family, entertainment, career)

Lesson 25: Sword Bargain

Warm up: Did you collect anything as a child? Do you collect anything now?

Vocabulary:

Treasure	You're killing me!	Steep
Price	Magnificent	Throw in (something)
Limited edition	Precious	Are you crazy?
Discount	Signature	Signed

Listening Comprehension  https://www.oneworldkorea.com/mc---beginner---session-3.html

Watch the video and listen for main ideas to fill in the blanks with vocabulary words.

Shopkeeper: Oh, I see you guys have found my little ________________ (sword from *Game of Thrones*).

Leonard: Yeah, it's okay. I guess.

Sheldon: Okay?! It's ___________________!

Leonard: *What do you want for it?*

Shopkeeper:: It's hard to put a ________________ on something that's a copy of something that was on paid cable. *For my friends, let's say* $250.

Leonard: Oh, that's pretty ________________.

Shopkeeper: It's a limited ________________. They only made 8,000 of these bad boys.

Sheldon: There's only 8,000. We're wasting precious time. Buy it.

Leonard: Hang on. *Can you do any better*?

Shopkeeper: Are you kidding?! I'm already giving you the friends and family discount.

Sheldon:: Oh, you hear that? We're getting the friends and family ________________. We are honored and we will take it.

- What do they want to buy?
- Do you think the price the shopkeeper is offering is too steep?
- Have you bought a "limited edition" item before?

Leonard: Slow down. $200.

Sheldon: What are you doing? 250 is already a discounted price!

Leonard: *Will you ______________ _________.*

Shopkeeper: I'll tell you what. I'll go 235.

Leonard: Nope, maybe ______________ time.

Shopkeeper: Okay 225. That's my final ________________.

Sheldon: Take it. Take it.

Leonard: 200.

Shopkeeper: Man, you're ________________ me!

Sheldon: He's killing you! I can't breathe.

Shopkeeper: 210 and I'm losing money.

Sheldon: Oh, now, we can't let him lose money, Leonard. I'm so ______________.

Leonard:: 210 and you throw in the Iron Man helmet.

Shopkeeper: Are you ______________? That helmet is signed by Robert Downey Jr.

Leonard: So?

- Do you prefer bargaining or paying a set price?
- What's the best price you've ever paid for something?
- Have you ever gotten a star to sign something for you?

Grammar Focus

1. Only

- ✓ Only can be an adjective to mean there is few of something
- ✓ As an adjective it is used in front of the noun.
- ✓ Only can be an adverb to mean something is limited
- ✓ As an adverb it can be placed at different spots to add emphasis

	Adjective Form Only + *Noun*	**Adverb Form** Only + <u>Verb</u> / <u>Modal</u> + Only + <u>Verb</u> / <u>Verb</u> + Only
Sentences	I am the **only** *customer* in the store. This is our **only** *one*. **Only** *8000 copies* were made.	This phone is **only** <u>sold</u> here. You <u>can</u> **only** <u>get</u> this price here. I want to <u>buy</u> **only**, not rent.
Questions	Are you the **only** *sales person*? Why is this **only** *10 dollars*?	Do you **only** <u>want</u> one? Why is it **only** <u>available</u> in blue?

<u>Practice:</u> In pairs, ask and answer the questions below using "only". Then ask follow up questions.

1. Are you the **only** *child* in your family?

2. Is it better to be the **only** *child* or have brothers and sisters?

3. Do you like to **only** <u>drink</u> one type of alcohol in a night or mix?

4. Is it unfair that **only** *women* can wear dresses?

5. If you <u>could</u> **only** <u>eat</u> one food for the rest of your life, what would you choose?

2. Bargaining Language

	Buyer	**Seller**
Starting	How much for that _______ (item)?	For you, I'll say $$$
Bargaining	That's too much. Can you do any better? How about $$$? Will you take $$$?	I'll give it to you for $$$ $$$ is as low as I can go. I'll give you the _______ discount $$$ is my final offer
Service	Can you throw in _______ (bonus item)?	I'll throw in _______ (bonus item)

Bargaining Role play

In pairs, act as a shopkeeper and customer. Use the bargaining language and your own creativity to negotiate a price for the items that are on sale below.

Single Person Car

3-Bedroom House

Newborn Puppy

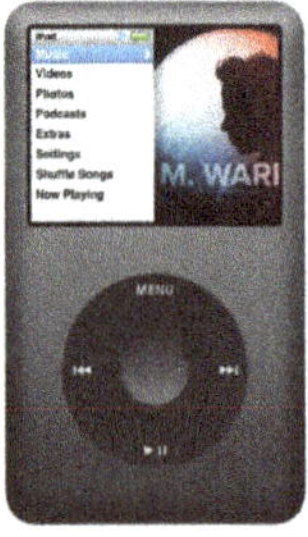

Video MP3 Player

Ironman Helmet

Diamond Ring

Men's Shoes

Jacket

Lesson 26: Wrong Directions

Warm up: Do you like to travel? Are you good with directions? Do you often get lost?

Vocabulary

Directions	Daydream	Fools
Straight	Statue	Actually
Left/Right	Wings	Appreciate
Block	Familiar	Honesty
Spot	Save	Crap
Wandering	Innocent	

Listening Comprehension 

Watch the video and listen for main ideas to fill in the blanks with vocabulary words.

Female Visitor: I'm so sorry. We're actually visiting from Canada and we're a bit lost.

Male Visitor: Yeah, would it be too much to ask you for directions?

Girl: No, ask away.

Male Visitor: Thank you, great.

Female Visitor: Well, we actually forgot the name of the _______________________.

Girl: _______________________________________ I don't know where anything is. I need directions just to get home from work every day. Why did I say yes? Could have easily said, "Nope, sorry." Why do I need to be liked?

Male Visitor: There's a big _________with ________.

Girl: ________with ________? That sounds ___________. I think I, I think I do know where this is. Wow, I'm going to save these innocent fools vacation.

Male Visitor: Are you okay?

Girl: Yeah, sorry, sorry... Yeah I totally know where that is actually. You're gonna go 10 ________________ _______________, you're gonna go four _____________ _______________, and then three ________________ __________________, and it's gonna be right there.

Female Visitor: Oh wonderful, thank you so much.

- Where are the travelers visiting from? What are they looking for?

Girl: Have fun, have fun in America. Crazy Canadians. Wait, that statue doesn't have wings. Oh no, I gave them the wrong directions. They're going to be so lost, _______________ for days.... Maybe I can fix this..... You guys, I'm so sorry. I don't know where that thing is. I _________________.

Female Visitor: We appreciate your _________________.

Male Visitor: Hey, do you want to be our best friend?

Girl: Yes! I do! .....Eh, I'm sure they will be fine.

- What did she do when she realized her mistake?

- Do you help strangers in trouble? Have you ever given bad directions?

- Where have you gotten lost? What did you do?

Grammar Focus

1. Prepositions of Place – IN, AT, ON

- ✓ The preposition comes before the Noun.
- ✓ Used to describe the location of places, buildings, and streets.

"In" general area, city, country or room/building	"At" exact position or specific place	On The top, Streets and sides
In London	At work	On the roof of my house
In America	At school	On the left side
In the department store	At the subway station	On the corner of 1st and 2nd Street

Practice 1: Use WH- questions to ask your partner the location of commonly known places. Answer using prepositions of place in full sentences.

Example: "Where is Avenue France?"

➔ "Avenue France is **next to** Lotte Mart and **around the corner from** Pangyo Station."

> **More Prepositions of Place**
>
> **Down the street** from the bank
>
> **Across from** Emart
>
> **Between** Seventh Street **and** Central Park
>
> **Around the corner from** Starbucks
>
> **Next to** the lake

2. Giving Directions

- ✓ Verb comes first when giving commands
- ✓ Use Action verbs such as **go/walk/drive/turn** with nouns of location

Turn Left then **turn right**

Go <u>two blocks</u>

Go <u>to the corner</u>

Go <u>past</u> the store

Go <u>straight</u>

Go <u>over the bridge</u>

Practice 2: Using the same locations from Practice 1, ask and give directions to those locations from where you are now.

Example: "How do I get to Avenue France from here?"

➔ Go out the main entrance of H-Square and **turn left. Turn right** at the corner. Then **go two blocks. Go over a bridge.** Then **turn left** and **walk one block**. Avenue France is on the right side.

Activity

We will play a game in pairs. One person will get a completed map from the teacher. The other will listen carefully and write answers in the blank map. The person with the map will give directions to the other. Take turns giving directions and listening. The goal is to fill the map as much as possible.

Remember to...

- ✓ Read slowly and clearly for your partner.
- ✓ Don't show your partner the answers, try to speak out any problems.
- ✓ **Use Where is the...? / How do I get to the ...?**

Example Practice:

"How do I get to the coffee shop **from** the bank?" ➜ "**Go straight one block**, then **turn left on** Main Street. **Go one more block** and it is the 2nd building **on your right**."

"Where is the post office?" ➜ "It's **next to** the high school and the bank."

City Map Locations

hospital	supermarket	theater
city hall	restaurant	church
fire station	park	temple
police station	zoo	subway station
coffee shop	gas station	bus station
hair salon	college	parking garage
post office	high school	soccer field
hotel	middle school	
shopping mall	elementary school	

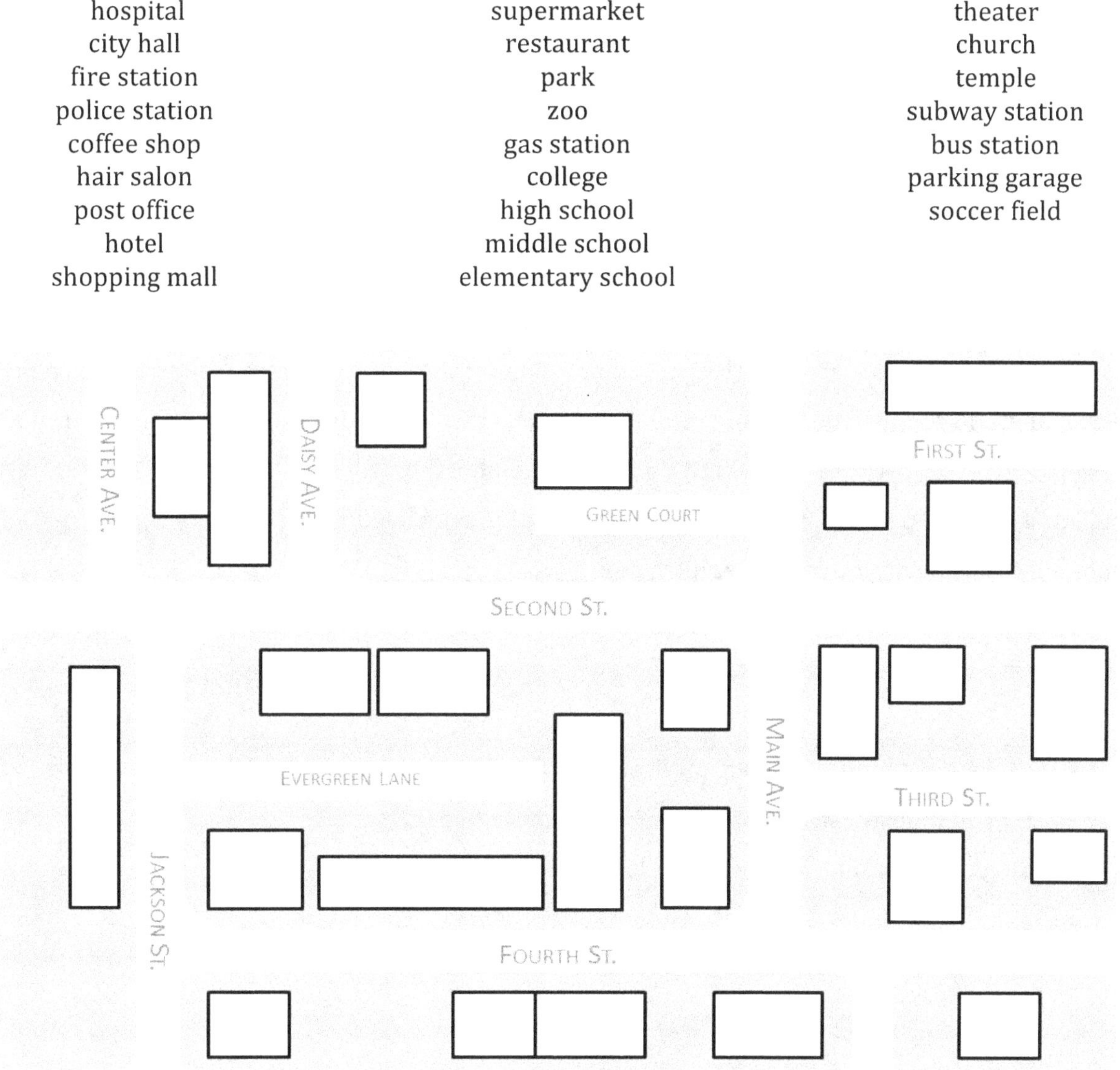

Lesson 27: Cheapest Places to Live

Warm up: How many times did you move in your lifetime?

Where did you live and where do you live now?

Vocabulary

upgrade	lifestyle	neglect
cash	price tag	maid service
spend	public transportation	household chores
homesickness	preoccupied	plenty

Listening Comprehension    https://www.oneworldkorea.com/mc---beginner---session-3.html

Watch the video and listen for main ideas to fill in the blanks with vocabulary words.

Number 5: Malaysia. With less than $300 monthly ______________ on a one bedroom apartment, you'll be sure to have plenty of cash to spend on whatever you like. If ______________ gets to you while in Malaysia, feel free to spend all of that extra cash at the country's largest shopping mall, "Times Square Mall." With 15 floors, a hotel, a bowling alley, and more than one Starbucks, it's almost as if you've never left home.

- How does the rent in Malaysia compare to your home country?

Number 3: Nicaragua. Because prices are so low in Central America's largest country, you could easily upgrade your lifestyle by moving to Nicaragua. It will cost you less than $10 to get around on __________________ every month, and a gym membership will only cost you $30 a month. Since you'll be **preoccupied** with keeping yourself entertained, you might **neglect** your __________________. No worries though. For $60, ______________ can swing through and clean up after you 3 times a week.

- Which services can you buy in Nicaragua?
- Do you think Nicaragua or Malaysia is better to live in?
- Do you think your home country is a cheap place to live?

Grammar Focus

"as adjective as"

- ✓ Use "as … as" to show that two things are equal
- ✓ Use "NOT + as … as" to show that two things are NOT equal

subject + be-verb + **as <u>adjective</u> as** object	subject + be-verb + **NOT as <u>adjective</u> as** object
The cat is **as <u>big</u> as** the Chihuahua. Sally is **as <u>beautiful</u> as** Kelly.	Chicago is**n't as <u>big</u> as** New York. Baby elephants are**n't as <u>cute</u> as** baby tigers.
subject + verb + **as <u>many/much noun</u> as object**	subject + **don't** verb + **as <u>many/much noun</u> as** object
Donald owns **as <u>many houses</u> as** Bill. He can eat **as <u>much food</u> as** a horse.	They **don't** play as **<u>many games</u> as** us. She **doesn't** earn as **<u>much money</u> as** Sarah.

Practice: Compare these two different images using "as … as" and the words below.

Nouns	Adjectives	Sentence:
Tree	Bright/Dark	The left tree is **not as** <u>dark</u> **as** the right tree.
Garage	Wide/narrow	____
Walkway	Straight/Curved	____
Chimney	Full/empty	____
Fence	Long/Short	____
Dog	Big/Small	____
Weather	Sunny/Cloudy	____

Adding Emphasis

✓ "Just" and "Almost" can be added before "as...as" to stress similarity
✓ "Quite" and "Nearly" can be added between "not" and "as...as" to stress difference

Similarities Just = (emphasis) Almost = (similar but not the same)	Differences Not quite = (small difference) Not nearly = (big difference)
The second Star Wars movie is ***just*** as <u>good</u> **as** the first.	Riding a bike is**n't** *quite* as **easy as** walking.
Bob watched ***just*** as <u>**many movies**</u> **as** me.	She **didn't** see *quite* as <u>**many animals**</u> **as** him.
Bees are ***almost*** as **dangerous as** Snakes.	Peaches are**n't** *nearly* as **delicious as** mangos.
Tyson bought ***almost*** as <u>**much gold**</u> **as** Arnold.	Tina **didn't** sleep *nearly* as <u>**much time**</u> **as** Andy.

Discussion:

Which amenities are most important to you? Using the adjectives "important" to practice using the adverbs: *nearly, quite, almost, just.* Ask and answer questions with a partner using the topics listed.

Example:
B: Which is more important to you, a swimming pool or a gym?
A: For me, a <u>swimming pool</u> is ***just* as important as** a <u>gym</u>, because my kids like to swim.
B: Really? For me, a <u>swimming pool</u> is**n't** *nearly* **as important as** a <u>gym</u>.
A: Why?
B: ...

<u>Location</u>
public transportation
traffic
restaurants
shopping
work place
noise

<u>Amenities</u>
security
parking lot
garden/outdoor areas
bathroom
park/playground
spa/pool
fitness center
pets allowed

<u>Appliances</u>
dishwasher
laundry machine
microwave
refrigerator
air conditioner
heater
built-in furniture

Lesson 28: If You Don't

Warm Up: What did you do for fun when you were a child?
What toys did you play with? Which were your favorite?

Vocabulary

Matches	Smash	Take care of
Permission	Rip apart	Launch
Find out	Confirm	Cookout
Blow up	Busted	Outcome

Listening Comprehension  https://www.oneworldkorea.com/mc---beginner---session-3.html

Watch the video and listen for main ideas to fill in the blanks with vocabulary words.

Sid (into speaker): Houston, All systems are go. Requesting permission to launch . . . Hey? How'd you get out here? Oh well. You and I can have a ______________ later. Houston, do we have permission to launch? Roger. ______________. You are confirmed at "T" minus ten seconds. And counting. Ten, nine, eight, seven, six, five, four, three, two, one...

Woody: Reach for the sky!

Sid: Huh?

Woody: This town ain't big enough for the two of us.

Sid: What?

Woody: Somebody's poisoned the water hole.

Sid: It's ______________.

Woody: Who are you calling busted, buster? That's right. I'm talking to you, Sid Phillips. We don't like being ______________, Sid. Or ______________ or ______________

Sid: "We"??

Woody: That's right! Your toys! From now on, you must ______________ good ______________ of your toys! Because <u>if you don't, we'll find out</u>, Sid. We toys can see everything. So play nice.

- Did you used to play with anything dangerous like matches?
- Did you take good care of your toys?
- What happens if you don't take care of...
    o A pet
    o A boyfriend/girlfriend
    o A car
    o Your health

Grammar Focus

"If" First Conditional

- ✓ The conditional clause is in present tense for first conditional
- ✓ Present tense is used to describe a *typical outcome*
- ✓ Future tense is used to describe a *probable outcome*
- ✓ Future words can include *will, be going to, might, could, want to, hope to*

If/When *A* **happens**, *B* **(usually) happens** present ↔ typical outcome	**If** *A* **happens**, *B* ***will*** **happen** present ↔ future outcome
If it <u>rains</u>, the game (usually) <u>is</u> cancelled.	**If** you <u>don't help</u> me, I'<u>*m going to*</u> cry.
When I <u>drink</u> coffee, I (usually) <u>can't sleep</u> well.	**If** he <u>goes</u> to the party, I *<u>won't</u>* go.
I <u>am</u> not a good worker, **if** I <u>don't sleep</u>.	**If** I <u>don't get</u> a promotion, I *<u>will quit</u>*.
I <u>give</u> money to my parents, **when** I <u>get</u> a bonus.	I *<u>might</u>* sing a song, **if** my team <u>wins</u>.
What <u>do</u> you do **if** you <u>are</u> hungry?	**What** *will* you do **if** you <u>lose</u> your job?

<u>Practice 1</u>: In pairs, finish the following sentences with your own ideas. Then ask follow up questions.

Example: A: When my favorite sports team wins, I celebrate with my friends.
B: Where do you celebrate?
A: We usually go to a chicken and beer restaurant near my house.
B: What is your favorite sports team?
A: The Chicago Cubs, of course!

<u>Typical Outcome</u>

1. When I drink too much coffee. . . .

2. When I have to wake up early. . . .

3. If I finish work late. . . .

4. If a person from you country wins an Olympic gold medal . . . .

5. If I am running late . . . .

<u>Probable Outcome</u>

1. If I get a promotion. . .

2. If I lose my job. . . .

3. If there is bad weather this weekend. . . .

4. I will be happy if . . . .

6. It will be nice if . . . .

<u>Practice 2</u>: Make First Conditional questions with the phrases "What do you do if..." or "What will you do if..." and using the pictures below. Then give answers and explain why.

Discussion

Read the list of social rules and check which ones you agree or disagree with. Then in pairs, discuss why you agree or disagree.

- ☐ If you break something in a store, you should pay for it.
- ☐ If an old person gets on a train, you should give them your seat.
- ☐ If you are sick, you should not go to work.
- ☐ If you receive your food before others, you should wait to eat it.
- ☐ If you are on an elevator, you should not fart.
- ☐ If you break up with someone, you should do it face-to-face.
- ☐ If see two strangers fighting, you should call the police.

Read the list of opinions and check which ones you agree or disagree with. Then in pairs, discuss why you agree or disagree.

- ☐ If you don't get married before 30, you should hurry!
- ☐ If someone has food in their teeth, you should tell them.
- ☐ If someone buys you something, you should buy them something more expensive.
- ☐ If you borrow money from a friend, you should pay it back with interest.
- ☐ If your parents ask you to do something, you must do it.
- ☐ If you are angry with someone, you should refuse to talk to them.
- ☐ If you are sleepy at work, you should go take a nap in the bathroom.

Lesson 29: Rules of Success

Warm up: What did your parents expect you to do in the past?

What do your parents expect you to do now?

Vocabulary:

Cut the crap	preparing	have a shot (at sth)
Society	to fit in	have a great run
rule	get into	get (accepted) into college
successful	accepted	
	cobbler	

Listening Comprehension  https://www.oneworldkorea.com/mc---beginner---session-3.html

Watch first: As you <u>watch the video</u>, listen and try to get the main ideas.

-   What news does Bartleby tell his parents?
-   How do his parents feel about this?

Listen for Details
Now listen again and fill in the blanks with vocabulary words as you listen.

Dad: Okay, cut the crap. Bartleby. Society has ______________. And the first rule is: You go to college.

Mom: Mmmhmm.

Dad: You want to have a happy and successful life? You go to college. If you want to be somebody, you go to college. If you want to ______________ in, you go to college.

Bartleby: Well, you know what? Maybe I didn't get into college.

Dad: What do you mean?

Bartleby: I didn't get ________________ anywhere.

Mom: Oh, Bartleby. I knew he should've started preparing for college in junior high, like his sister.

Dad: Now, she's got a ________________.

Younger sister: I've got a shot.

Mom: She's got a shot.

Bartleby: Listen, guys. There are plenty of __________________ people who didn't go to college. Albert Einstein, you know. Pocahontas never went to college. Corey Feldman and Corey Haim. They had a great run. Both Lewis and Clark. Suzanne Somers. Bono.

Mom: I need to go check on the ________________.

Bartleby: "Check the cobbler" Glug, glug, glug.

Dad: You know, I really don't care what Sonny Bono did or didn't do. You're going to college.

-   Do you think your parents would feel the same way as Bartleby's parents?

-   How important is college acceptance in your culture?

-   What do you think Bartleby should do?

Grammar Focus:

"If" Second Conditional

- ✓ This is referred to as the "unreal" conditional, because it is used with fantasy situations that are currently not true and have a high possibility of not becoming true
- ✓ The conditional clause is in *past tense*
- ✓ The outcome clause uses *"would + verb"*

If *A* **happened**, *B **would*** happen	
past ↔ would + base V	
Question	**Answer**
If you <u>found</u> a bag full of money, **what** <u>would</u> you <u>do</u>?	**If** I <u>found</u> a bag full of money, I <u>would run</u> away quickly.
Who <u>would</u> you <u>meet</u>, **if** you <u>could meet</u> any celebrity?	**I** <u>would meet</u> Brad Pitt, **if** I <u>could meet</u> any celebrity.
If you <u>could travel</u> anywhere for free, **where** <u>would</u> you <u>travel</u>?	**If** I <u>could travel</u> anywhere for free, I <u>would go</u> to Antarctica because I like penguins.

<u>Practice 1:</u> In pairs, finish the following questions with your own ideas. Then ask follow up questions.

Example: A: If you won the lottery. . . . who would you share your money with?
B: I wouldn't share it with anyone!
A: Really? What about your parents?
B: First I would buy an island. Then I would invite my parents to live with me.
A: Where would you buy an island?
B: . . . .

1. If aliens attacked earth . . . .

2. If you could travel to outer space . . . .

3. If you had a time machine . . . .

4. If you had enough money that you didn't need to work. . . .

5. If there was a medicine that made you live forever . . . .

6. If you could download skills directly to your brain . . . .

<u>Practice 2:</u> Make Second Conditional questions with the phrases "What would you do if..." and using the pictures below. Then give answers and explain why.

Discussion:

Check which ideas you agree with. Then discuss why you agree or disagree.

If a young person doesn't go to college...

- ☐ they won't make money
- ☐ they won't fit in
- ☐ their life will be happier
- ☐ they won't have a successful life
- ☐ they will save money
- ☐ they will start their career earlier

If a person wants to be successful...

- ☐ they should be really smart
- ☐ they should get a job at a big company
- ☐ they should become a CEO
- ☐ they should get married
- ☐ they should have 3 or more kids
- ☐ they should live a healthy life style
- ☐ they should have good relationships with friends and family
- ☐ they should be kind and generous to others

Lesson 30: Product Review

Warm Up: Do you usually read reviews before you buy something?

Vocabulary

Product	Post	A ton
Pretty much	Coupon	Mouth
Vacuum	Stoked	Awesome
Feed	Fulltime	Entire
Amazing	Shed	Completely
Interview		Efficiency

Listening Comprehension  https://www.oneworldkorea.com/mc---beginner---session-3.html

Watch the video and listen for main ideas to fill in the blanks with vocabulary words.

So this product pretty much ___________ my life. I'm able to vacuum while I'm sleeping. I'm able to vacuum while I'm ___________ the baby. It's pretty amazing, and I want to tell you about it. Hi my name is Diane and I'm doing an interview about the iRobot because I saw someone post it on Facebook and I thought for some reason that they weren't very good. So I've never though about them and this person that posted it said it was ___________. So I thought I should check it out for myself and it just so happens that *Bed Bath and Beyond* will take a 20% ___________ on these things so I was stoked to try one out.

-   What are some things that Diane can do while vacuuming?
-   What two things made Diane decide to buy the iRobot?
-   Have you seen the iRobot before? Do you want to have one?

I'm a fulltime working mom and my husband works ____________. We have two dogs, one that ___________ a ton, and my little son is walking around everywhere just putting everything in his ___________. So we have to make sure that the house stays pretty clean.

-   Why does Diane need the iRobot? Listen for 4 reasons.
-   What are some reasons why you might need the iRobot?

And there's nothing more awesome than being able to play with your child in one room and have this little robot vacuum an ___________ other room. So by the time I go back in there, it's completely clean. It's great!

Useful Phrases

1. "There's nothing more adjective"

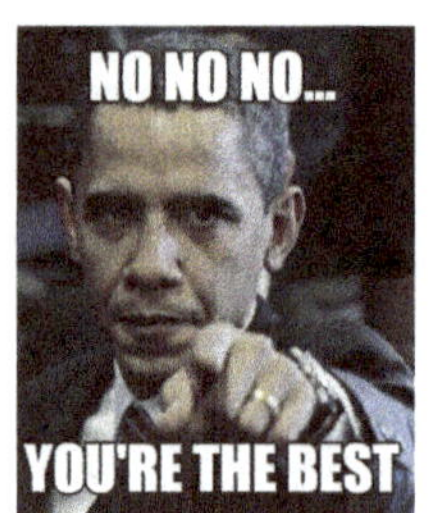

✓ This phrase means that something is the best or the top rank

Structure: "There is nothing <u>more</u> **adjective** than **verb+ing or noun**"

<u>Example 1:</u> There is nothing <u>more</u> **exciting** than **riding a motorcycle**.

<u>Example 2:</u> There is nothing **bigger** than **a whale**.

Practice: In pairs, try to use this expression with the ideas below.

Friendly	+	Animal _______________________________________
Amazing	+	Movie _______________________________________
Famous	+	Star _______________________________________
Interesting	+	Activity _______________________________________

2. Expressing a Reason of Efficiency

✓   This structure can be used to show that two things can be done at the same time

Structure: (Subject) **is/am/are + able to** <u>verb</u>   **while** (Subject) **is/am/are** <u>verb+ing</u>

<u>Example 1:</u>   I **am able to** <u>vacuum</u>   **while** I **am** <u>sleeping</u>.

<u>Example 2:</u>   They **are able to** <u>drink</u> water   **while** they **are** <u>running</u>.

Practice: In pairs, think of two things that people can do at the same time with these products:

<u>Example:</u> MP3 Player ➔ People **are able to** <u>listen</u> to music **while** they **are** <u>running</u>.

Google Glass _______________________________ while _______________________________

Smart Phone _______________________________ while _______________________________

Driverless Car _______________________________ while _______________________________

Waterproof camera _______________________________ while _______________________________

3. Expressing a Reason of Purpose

- ✓ This structure can be used to show a positive use of something

Structure: (subject) **is/am/are** <u>positive adjective</u> **for** <u>verb + ing</u>

<u>Example 1:</u>   iRobot **is** <u>great</u> **for** <u>cleaning</u> dog hair.

<u>Example 2:</u>   The Internet **is** <u>useful</u> **for** <u>finding</u> information.

Practice: In pairs, ask and answer questions about the following products:

<u>Example:</u> MP3 Player ➜ A: What do you use an iWatch for?

B: An iWatch is great for seeing phone messages.

- ➢ Coffee Machine
- ➢ Xbox
- ➢ Toothpaste
- ➢ Air conditioner
- ➢ Mask & Goggles
- ➢ Bluetooth headphones

Activity: Product Review Interview

In pairs tell your partner about one product that you own, which you really like and one product that you don't like.

- ✓ Try to use the useful phrases from this lesson
- ✓ Explain the positive and negative reasons for liking that product.
- ✓ Take notes on your partner's response and be ready to tell the class about your partner's product reviews.
- ✓ Ask each other follow up questions to get more details. Consider the questions below:

- ☐ Where did you buy this product?
- ☐ How much does it cost?
- ☐ What is it used for?
- ☐ What else can you do while using this product?
- ☐ Is there nothing better than this product?

**Brian Devine** is an American educator who has been teaching and developing English education curriculums since 2005. During his time pursuing a master's degree in education at Seattle University, he became a Washington State certified teacher in English Language Arts and Social Studies. He taught in the Seattle Public School district and in an ESL program associated with Seattle Pacific University. In 2010, he took a position as a Language Arts and Social Studies teacher at an international school in South Korea where he became a specialist in curriculum design and a leader in blending traditional educational methods with modern technology. He is also the co-founder and director of One World Language, an online platform that provides language-learning curriculum.

Media & Culture

Research, Writing & Editing

This book is a collection of topics and materials gathered from various published resources and internet materials.
Original sources for the videos are posted on the One World website on the study resource page.
Special thanks to Maia Harrell and Roseann Orthober, instructors at One World Language, for research and writing original drafts for several lessons.